Social Media for WordPress
Beginner's Guide

A quicker way to build communities, engage members, and promote your site

Michael Kuhlmann

PUBLISHING

BIRMINGHAM - MUMBAI

Social Media for WordPress
Beginner's Guide

First published: April 2012

Production Reference: 1160412

Published by Packt Publishing Ltd.
Livery Place
35 Livery Street
Birmingham B3 2PB, UK.

ISBN 978-1-84719-980-5

www.packtpub.com

Cover Image by Michael Kuhlmann (mike@epictum.com)

Credits

Author

Michael Kuhlmann

Reviewers

David Hopkins

Derek Key

Adii Pienaar

Acquisition Editor

Robin de Jongh

Lead Technical Editor

Kedar Bhat

Technical Editor

Apoorva Bolar

Project Coordinator

Alka Nayak

Proofreader

Mario Cecere

Indexer

Rekha Nair

Production Coordinator

Arvindkumar Gupta

Cover Work

Arvindkumar Gupta

Foreword

One of the most amazing statistics I have ever read, I read while reading this book—*15 percent of the web now runs on WordPress.*

The impact of this statistic is staggering. The size of that two-digit percentage, when multiplied by the entire Internet is so vast as to be incomprehensible. Yet the bigger imponderable the greater statistic comes when we realize that 100 percent minus 15 percent is 85 percent. That 85 percent has yet to discover WordPress.

In my career, I deal with web statistics every day. At Packt we publish books on IT and web technologies, and so it is to the web that we go for our research to base our assumptions of what is popular, what is worth spending our time, and an author's time on the technologies that will sell books. WordPress is virtually unique in that its popularity grows steeply and almost linearly over time, right from day one, and has done so for the last eight years, up, up, and up. Eating up the Internet bit by bit like an unstoppable virus. One might be forgiven for thinking the whole of that other 85 percent might succumb given time.

When setting up a content based website the fact of the matter is that there is no longer a reason not to use WordPress. Drupal and Joomla! have had their day and are declining in popularity. WordPress has now won the battle of the CMS outright. And the reason is simple. With a few tweaks and a five-minute installation, WordPress is the most search engine-friendly way to put content on the web bar. Yesterday that was enough to get you noticed on the web. Today, WordPress is only half the story. The other half is social media. And that's where Michael's book comes in.

When you begin to combine WordPress with Social Media elements you have the power of the Internet at your disposal; a way to fully engage readers; and that's a concept as staggering as the one we started with. Michael is a true expert and has written a book that is a pure joy to read because it gives you and me the tools we need to succeed where we may have failed before, yet without cost or high-level skills. The plan of action contained herein is, simply put, a template for web success that anyone can follow. I couldn't commend this book more emphatically to anyone who needs to be heard above the deafening noise of the Internet and nowadays that probably means all of us.

Robin de Jongh
Acquisition Editor, WordPress Social Media and WordPress Marketing

About the Author

Michael Kuhlmann is a writer, entrepreneur, and web designer who specializes in WordPress and BuddyPress development. He has worked nearly 10 years in the publishing industry and has written a handful of tutorials spanning topics from print design to web design. To date, his BuddyPress themes have been downloaded more than 100,000 times.

He serves as the director of web design for Thompson Media Group, a publishing company, where he oversees seven brands and their respective web properties and marketing collateral. In 2008, he co-founded `http://avenuek9.com`, a pet site catering to canine lovers and their furry friends, which garnered the attention of The Huffington Post and *Perez Hilton*. His latest offering comes in the form of a WordPress hosting service `http://joinevo.com`, which is a mobile-friendly WordPress platform and marketing service.

Prior to becoming a web designer, he served as a managing and news editor for a San Diego newspaper. His work has been published in The New York Times, The San Diego Business Journal, and The San Diego Union-Tribune among other notable publications.

This book is dedicated to my amazing wife Shannon and our precious daughter Lily. I would also like to thank my family, friends, book editors, and all the dog owners at Morse Park for your continued support. You are all awesome!

Last, this book would not have been possible without all the editors involved—Adii Pienaar, Kedar Bhat, David Hopkins, Derek Key, and Robin de Jongh. If we all didn't live in separate time zones, I'd take us all out for drinks. Thanks guys!

About the Reviewers

David Hopkins is a regular blogger on aspects of social media, social networks, learning technology, and general blogging activities and techniques. He started his current blogging activity in 2008 but was an advocate of blogging and online communities from a far back as 1999 and his first role as a web designer.

Using advances in social media websites and online social networks, David has made the most of what is available and has grown an International reputation for his blogging and conference activity.

You can follow David on his eLearning Blog (www.dontwasteyourtime.co.uk) and Twitter (@hopkinsdavid) where he writes on aspects of eLearning, technology, social media, and social networks.

Derek Key is currently a member of the business development team at Schipul—the web marketing company. He has worn many hats at Schipul from account executive, to customer support to now being a key member of the business development department. He's no stranger to getting knee-deep in project management and navigating the technical trenches of the various CMS software used to create amazing websites for his clients.

Derek has a wide range of experience, from marketing for the web, print, TV, and radio, to business development. He hails from the University of Texas, where he majored in advertising and has a minor in business foundations.

His love for all things techie dates back to his days in high school. Besides learning and exploring new possibilities online, and helping clients grow their businesses, Derek is a photography addict (www.derekskey.com), music fanatic, and football fan.

Adii Pienaar is an entrepreneur, husband, and very new father; the combination of these roles resulting in an epic and challenging journey. Unlike the bio's of most serial entrepreneurs, Adii is (as at the time of this going to press) a one-hit wonder with his role as co-founder of *WooThemes*. That status isn't for a lack of trying either; it's just that the other attempts lost more money than they made.

Adii is a bit of a rebel at heart (in his previous online iteration, he dubbed himself as *Adii Rockstar*) and absolutely loves challenges. His latest, professional challenge is getting rid of the one-hit wonder moniker and moving to the higher echelons of serial entrepreneurship. As such, you'll always find Adii dabbling in the odd side-project (such as, *The Rockstar Foundation*), advising/mentoring, other startup founders, or getting his toes wet in angel investing. He further harbors the dream of being an A-list blogger and has even tried to augment that reputation by publishing his debut book—*Rockstar Business*.

Adii believes that there is a fine balance between ambition, working hard, and spending time on the important things in life. As a result, he has recently realized that he actually wants to work less instead of more without having to compromise on his goals and ambitions in life. Add all of these ingredients into one life and you find yourself watching a startup/ entrepreneurs-version of *The Bold & The Beautiful*.

www.PacktPub.com

Support files, eBooks, discount offers and more

You might want to visit www.PacktPub.com for support files and downloads related to your book.

Did you know that Packt offers eBook versions of every book published, with PDF and ePub files available? You can upgrade to the eBook version at www.PacktPub.com and as a print book customer, you are entitled to a discount on the eBook copy. Get in touch with us at service@packtpub.com for more details.

At www.PacktPub.com, you can also read a collection of free technical articles, sign up for a range of free newsletters and receive exclusive discounts and offers on Packt books and eBooks.

http://PacktLib.PacktPub.com

Do you need instant solutions to your IT questions? PacktLib is Packt's online digital book library. Here, you can access, read and search across Packt's entire library of books.

Why Subscribe?

- ◆ Fully searchable across every book published by Packt
- ◆ Copy and paste, print and bookmark content
- ◆ On demand and accessible via web browser

Free Access for Packt account holders

If you have an account with Packt at www.PacktPub.com, you can use this to access PacktLib today and view nine entirely free books. Simply use your login credentials for immediate access.

Table of Contents

Preface

The decision to write a book about this content management system was an easy one. At the time of this writing, WordPress powers more than 15 percent of all websites online. That's a considerable bite out of the Internet. Unfortunately, that also meant a lot of books had already been published on WordPress. After a couple of weeks, mulling over what this book should be about, I decided to tackle the popular topic of social media.

The book you're holding was originally centered on **BuddyPress** (**BP**), a WordPress plugin that extends your site's functionality by adding a social layer a la Facebook to create user profiles, add friends, send private messages, join and create groups, and so on. It wasn't a horrible idea. There were, however, several setbacks to solely dedicating an entire book to one plugin.

The vast majority of Internet users, let alone WordPress users, aren't familiar with this plugin. Unlike the words *social media*, which are constantly being tossed around in news headlines, BP hasn't had its shining moment yet. Another big setback to a BP-specific book revolved around the timeliness of the content. With the ever-maturing code, there was a good chance for the book to be out-dated before it even hit the shelves. But the biggest reason not to write it just on BP was that it demanded many resources. You'd need a significant amount of time to manage not only your site but also your members. You'd also need to run your site on a dedicated server, once you reached a large volume of traffic or risk downtime on a shared server. In either case, you'd need a bigger annual budget and lots of patience. This was just one trifecta of a crapshoot I didn't want to mess with. Compromise? I wrote one chapter (the longest one) on BP and focused the remaining chapters on social media marketing techniques. It seemed the best of both worlds.

Confession—I don't claim to be a social media guru, ninja, or wizard, and I'm not the biggest proponent of social media. Sometimes, it just annoys me. Do I want to *Like* or *+1* every nook and cranny of a website? No! There's a fine balance between just right and over-the-top. The tested-and-tried activities outlined in this book exemplify this approach by letting you mix the various marketing techniques, the newsletters, forums, and BP components, for example, that promote the social interactions.

Social Media for WordPress also covers site management and web analytics, as handling those two areas are essential to running any site and campaign. After all, you can't improve what you can't measure. Finally, this book utilizes a myriad of plugins, which have been specifically chosen because of their popularity, ratings, and support. For all the times you don't want to deal with snarky support, you can opt for dedicated paid support that's kind and timely. The research has already been done for you. You're welcome. Last, since this is a continuing effort on social media marketing, you can visit the dedicated site at http://socialmediaforwp.com or scan the following code:

(You'll learn how to create this in Chapter 7)

What this book covers

Chapter 1, *Share it the Easy Way*, introduces you to the fundamentals, misconceptions, and basic implementations of social media. You'll also learn about some native WordPress features that drive more site engagement.

Chapter 2, *Building the Social Network: BuddyPress and WP Symposium*, teaches you how to roll out your social media layer with BuddyPress and add game-like capabilities to help you engage your site members.

Chapter 3, *Community Forums for the Masses*, is devoted to bbPress and BuddyPress, showing you how to automatically publish WordPress posts to Twitter using RSS feeds.

Chapter 4, *VIP Memberships*, incorporates the social media aspect through site memberships and the concept of gamification. You'll find out how to create category-specific content restrictions, which are applicable only to non-members.

Chapter 5, *Keeping Up with the Stats*, implements Google Analytics to help you track your social media efforts and gauge their effectiveness.

Chapter 6, *Managing your Site*, let's you discover some shortcuts to managing content by showing you how to publish posts through e-mail. You'll also learn how to back up your site to avoid a social media meltdown.

Chapter 7, *Beyond the Plugins Towards True Engagement,* delves further into social media marketing automation by teaching you how to automatically post tweets, so you can spend more time on genuine dialogues and less time on producing relevant tweets.

What you need for this book

As this is a book for beginners, you will only need WordPress installed on your server and an FTP client, such as FileZilla. In some cases, you may need server access, which a web-host administrator can provide you with. The activities outlined in each chapter do not require any programming skills.

Who this book is for

This book is designed for WordPress users who would like to open the social floodgates to their sites. You do not need to be a WordPress expert, PHP developer, or social media maven to understand the material discussed in this book. However, having a firm grasp on WordPress basics and social networking sites is beneficial.

Conventions

In this book, you will find several headings appearing frequently.

To give clear instructions of how to complete a procedure or task, we use:

Time for action – heading

1. Action 1
2. Action 2
3. Action 3

Instructions often need some extra explanation so that they make sense, so they are followed with:

What just happened?

This heading explains the working of tasks or instructions that you have just completed.

You will also find some other learning aids in the book, including:

Pop quiz – heading

These are short multiple choice questions intended to help you test your own understanding.

Have a go hero – heading

These set practical challenges and give you ideas for experimenting with what you have learned.

You will also find a number of styles of text that distinguish between different kinds of information. Here are some examples of these styles, and an explanation of their meaning.

Code words in text are shown as follows: "Depending on your server permissions, you may receive another prompt to create a `bb-config.php file`, which you can easily create using Notepad (or TextEdit for OSX) and upload using FileZilla."

A block of code is set as follows:

```
<div id="countdowncontainer">
<script type="text/javascript">
var futuredate=new cdtime("countdowncontainer", "December 12, 2012
12:12:12")
futuredate.displaycountdown("days", formatresults)
</script>
</div>
```

New terms and **important words** are shown in bold. Words that you see on the screen, in menus or dialog boxes for example, appear in the text like this: " To enable rewards points for registrations and logins, navigate to **Modules** under **CubePoints** and click on the **Activate** link for the **Daily Points** module."

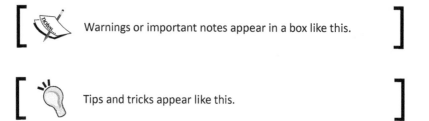

Warnings or important notes appear in a box like this.

Tips and tricks appear like this.

Reader feedback

Feedback from our readers is always welcome. Let us know what you think about this book—what you liked or may have disliked. Reader feedback is important for us to develop titles that you really get the most out of.

To send us general feedback, simply send an e-mail to feedback@packtpub.com, and mention the book title via the subject of your message.

If there is a topic that you have expertise in and you are interested in either writing or contributing to a book, see our author guide on www.packtpub.com/authors.

Customer support

Now that you are the proud owner of a Packt book, we have a number of things to help you to get the most from your purchase.

Downloading the example code for this book

You can download the example code files for all Packt books you have purchased from your account at http://www.PacktPub.com. If you purchased this book elsewhere, you can visit http://www.PacktPub.com/support and register to have the files e-mailed directly to you.

Errata

Although we have taken every care to ensure the accuracy of our content, mistakes do happen. If you find a mistake in one of our books—maybe a mistake in the text or the code—we would be grateful if you would report this to us. By doing so, you can save other readers from frustration and help us improve subsequent versions of this book. If you find any errata, please report them by visiting http://www.packtpub.com/support, selecting your book, clicking on the **errata submission form** link, and entering the details of your errata. Once your errata are verified, your submission will be accepted and the errata will be uploaded on our website, or added to any list of existing errata, under the Errata section of that title. Any existing errata can be viewed by selecting your title from http://www.packtpub.com/support.

Piracy

Piracy of copyright material on the Internet is an ongoing problem across all media. At Packt, we take the protection of our copyright and licenses very seriously. If you come across any illegal copies of our works, in any form, on the Internet, please provide us with the location address or website name immediately so that we can pursue a remedy.

Please contact us at copyright@packtpub.com with a link to the suspected pirated material.

We appreciate your help in protecting our authors, and our ability to bring you valuable content.

Questions

You can contact us at questions@packtpub.com if you are having a problem with any aspect of the book, and we will do our best to address it.

1
Share it the Easy Way

The process to make content easier to share and more engaging online doesn't have to be a complicated one. In fact, you don't even need the expertise of a professional web developer or a great amount of time for development. In a lot of instances, you can take existing components and mould them to your specific needs. You do, however, need to think creatively at times and be willing to stay persistent in learning how to accomplish your goals.

In this chapter, we shall:

♦ Go over what you should already know prior to reading this book

♦ Gain insight to social media and its benefits

♦ Learn the fundamentals, misconceptions, and basic implementations of social media

♦ Leverage WordPress's core features to drive more site engagement

♦ Create a newsletter campaign using a keyword-based RSS feed

♦ Explore ideas to build business relationships

So let's get on with it.

Before you read this book

This book assumes that you already have a fair understanding of WordPress, blogging, and social networking sites like Facebook, LinkedIn, and Twitter among others. It is not a book on how to build such networking sites but rather a primer on how you can provide your site visitors with similar site features, to drive more interactions with each other. Parts of this book will also rely on reputable third-party components and services to beef up your site.

You will also need to run a self-hosted version of WordPress that you can access on the backend, meaning that you can upload and modify files, which usually requires access to an FTP client, as well. Alternatively, you can easily get the same setup through services like ManageWP (`http://managewp.com`) or Pagely (`http://page.ly`), which bypass most of the technicalities. If you only understood half of the material thus far, you can brush up your knowledge through the resources listed below.

- Everything you need to know about WordPress:
  `http://codex.wordpress.org/Main_Page`

- Tutorials: `http://wordpress.tv/category/how-to/`,
  `http://wpmututorials.com/category/basics/`,
  `http://net.tutsplus.com/category/tutorials/wordpress/`

- WordPress news: `http://wordpress.org/news/`, `http://wpcandy.com`,
  `http://wpmu.org/`, `http://wptavern.com`

A brief overview of social media

Social media can spark a country's revolution, transform the way we educate ourselves, and drum up support for disaster relief. While there is no set definition shared by dictionaries, encyclopedias, or industry leaders, social media can be summarized as digital content that is cultivated online using mass communication applications such as Facebook, Twitter, and WordPress. There is room for granularity, of course, but attempting to break down the two ominous buzzwords is like defining the word *music*—it has so much scope and depth, and means different things to different people. Hence, social media is much easier to look at as a strategic game of prediction revolving around what tools to provide your audience for communicating and exchanging facts, figures, and other data. It is the answer to the question, *how can I establish a meaningful dialog?*

When Wael Ghonim set out to organize a revolution in Egypt, he was armed with a Facebook account and a plan. He launched Kullena Khaled Said (*We Are All Khaled Said*), a Facebook group, which solicited ideas for pro-democracy demonstrations and sought accountability for the unwrongful death of a 28 year old man who had been killed by the Egyptian security officials. The site gained so much momentum that former President Hosni Mubarak blocked the entire social networking site, thereby, sparking a revolution, which ultimately led to an uprising and his departure.

When educator and Harvard MBA graduate Salman Khan posted math tutorials on YouTube, they gained so much momentum that they ultimately formed the basis for his non-profit Khan Academy (`http://www.khanacademy.org`), where his mini-lectures have logged more than six million views worldwide. This social media movement that changed the political regime and drove the free Ivy League education was also easily identifiable during the 8.9-magnitude Japan earthquake in 2011, which resulted in a global humanitarian relief effort. Once the public discovered the vast amount of damage through a barrage of Facebook updates, YouTube videos, tweets, and other outlets, this set in motion a collective need to provide donations. The emergence of such innovative ideas in utilizing social connections, to effect change all converge back to establishing a genuine dialog.

Social media is the new Web 2.0

On new year's eve 1999, there was ample news coverage of what the cumulative effect could be in anticipation of January 1, 2000. Disasters would strike and riots would ensue as computers would not be able to roll over to the new millennium. It was known as the **Y2K bug**. But programs were checked and updated, and life carried on with everyday normalcy. Fast-forward several years and the term **Web 2.0** starts to gain traction. The buzzword trend continues with news and magazine outlets heralding headlines with Web 2.0 in them like it was the dawn of a new millennium. Yet in both the Y2K and Web 2.0 cases, there was no significant or drastic change in how people interacted with each other and there was no change in the content either.

Sure, social media and technologies have changed the delivery and rate, at which data transfers from point A to point B, but the protocol by which that occurs remains the same. A person has an intention of seeking or supplying information, or data, and determines the easiest path to carry out the action. These are the basics of any form of communication; **social technology**—web applications such as Facebook, Twitter, WordPress, and so on have simply improved on this by providing more gateways to make this digital data more transferable.

Going social does not mean going viral

A common misconception is that adding social media gadgets, badges, and other gizmos to a site will equate a considerable increase in unique page views or guarantee content going viral. This logic is false. It is as accurate as assuming a car will drive twice as fast on premium gasoline than on regular gasoline. The increase in page views is dependent on the relevancy, frequency, and originality of your content much like the acceleration of a car is dependent on the make, model, and year.

Content is king goes the old adage, but that is also only a part of the equation, since content in the wrong context will not solely drive social connections online. The content that gets spotlighted, re-tweeted, re-purposed, pinged back, and otherwise magnified under the scope of a mass audience has to matter first. It's the catchy headline, the intriguing picture, and the stimulating story that leaves the audience salivating. The content can be high-brow or low-brow, scientific or salacious, and any other number of combinations, but the data has to matter to its audience. Your readers have to decide if your content is worth pushing the **Like** button, for example, in order to relay that data to the next person. Social media, in this aspect, merely means providing the necessary tools to facilitate this type of action.

There are a myriad ways of going social. No rule book exists for providing the necessary tools to establish a meaningful dialog. Different websites have different demographics and goals, so what may work on one site may not fare well on your own site. In most cases, starting off with the simplest approach is often the best. A hyper-local community website called *yeah! Hackney* (`http://yeahhackney.com`), for example, utilizes a WordPress plugin called **BuddyPress (BP)** to enable members to create profiles, where they can access and discuss information about exciting events and places in Hackney, London. The site enables members to post status updates, send private messages, update profiles, join and create groups and more. Suffice to say you will learn more about BP-powered sites in the next chapter.

The WordPress advantage

With WordPress now powering 14.7 million sites, or nearly 15 percent of the entire web, including CNN, *The New York Times* and Lance Armstrong's LIVESTRONG foundation (`http://blog.livestrong.org`), many site users and visitors have already become familiar with its native functions, even if they don't know what they're called. WordPress ships with three core functions, or capabilities that are native to the application, which allow your users and consumers to establish a dialog, based on the data that is provided. They include the following:

- content syndication
- content update services
- a commenting system

It's easy to gloss over these basic features, as they have been part of the **Content Management System (CMS)** for a long time. There is a natural tendency to view social media as the lump sum of social networking sites like Facebook, MySpace, or LinkedIn. The expectation is that photo tagging, @mentioning, or group discussions are the key to driving social interactions online. However, the main distinction is that they are generally the key once site have garnered repeat site vistors who actively community engage with the site.

Doing more with core functions

Three key players of the tech world—Google, Apple Inc, and Microsoft, thought of seemingly brilliant ideas until they were lambasted as major flops. They included Google Wave, Ping, and the Zune. None of these projects were detrimental to the continued success of their respective companies.

WordPress has a similar weakness. Because of the sheer amount of extensions that are available to you, it's a simple system that you can make very bulky and complicated within a few mouse clicks. It's easy to get lost in a pool of plugins, because each one sounds better than the next, and with the web running at warp speed, it would seem beneficial to activate them all as soon as you can get your hands on them. However, a comment rating plugin, for example, isn't going to do much if hardly anybody leaves comments. A **Real Simple Syndication(RSS)** subscriber counter will look sad if only five people are subscribed to your site. You have to excel at the basics first to see your content thrive just like you need to have a firm understanding of WordPress before activating countless plugins

The karma of pingbacks and comments

Pingbacks and comments can work like little packs of karma. Using Ping-O-Matic natively, WordPress notifies you that your content has been linked to from another user on a different site. This typically happens in the form of a comment or post reply. You write an awesome post and a site visitor reads that post, prompting him or her to write a response and linking back to you. Plugins such as **subscribe to comments** can certainly add more engagement to let subscribers connect with you by getting notified every time there is a new comment on your awesome post, thereby, tempting them to write a new comment on your site. But it shouldn't stop there. You have to be proactive about your pingbacks and comments. Take the time to thank each commenter individually to let them know you care about his or her opinions regardless of whether they're good or bad. This is the equivalent of thanking guests for attending your party after they leave. It lets them feel more appreciated so they'll return. In contrast, deleting comments should also be discouraged, as it appears that your site is censoring or hiding content.

Food for thought: RSS feed basics

Content syndication can make a big difference. The beauty of WordPress is that it automatically produces a separate RSS feed for each category that you create (`http://www.yourdomain.tld/category/category-name/feed/`). Each site also has its main feed that includes all content (`http://www.yourdomain.tld/feed/`). Moreover, comments can be subscribed to just as easily (`http://www.yourdomain.tld/comments/feed/`). Even custom post types can have their individual feeds. This is important to remember, because each one of these feeds can be marketed as its own channel of information like a newsletter, without the extra effort. All mobile site visitors are able to use their feed readers, subscribe to a particular feed, and view the site content as if it was specifically tailored to them. You only need to provide your visitors with the feed link and a prominent wording for them to subscribe. The call to action is a simple yet crucial step, since they will not hunt down your RSS feeds by themselves; you have to spoon-feed your visitors.

Time for action – building an automated newsletter with a keyword-based RSS feed

Promoting your site content using RSS feeds is great, but what's even better is providing your site visitors with an easily accessible way to keep up with a particular trend or topic of your niche site. This allows your site visitors to skip a few steps by bypassing the search for the best RSS feed reader, the application installation itself, reading usage directions, and having to manually filter through a bunch of posts on a specific topic. Using a newsletter is more user-friendly, because it ensures your subscribers the delivery of relevant content by doing something they do on a regular basis such as checking the inbox. All your visitors have to do is fill out a form that subscribes them to your newsletter. Best of all, everything will be automated including the newsletter content aggregation, and delivery of the newsletter e-mails.

In this in-depth activity, you will learn how to provide your site visitors with information on the keyword **Mullenweg**. It contains three main parts:

◆ creating a subscriber signup form

◆ creating a keyword-based RSS feed

◆ creating a custom MailChimp newsletter campaign

Let's get started.

Part 1—creating a subscriber signup form

We'll use a popular third-party **Email Service Provider (ESP)** called MailChimp to send out the newsletter, so log on to `http://www.mailchimp.com` and register for a free account, if you don't already have one.

1. In your MailChimp dashboard, click on **create a subscriber list** and fill out all the required fields and name the list `Matt Mullenweg Newsletter` or something that describes your newsletter's topic or keyword.

2. Now, create a form that let's your site visitors sign up for your newsletter by clicking on **create a signup form**. (You should see this option in the next step. If you don't, click on **Dashboard | design signup forms**.)

3. MailChimp will automatically produce a basic **Signup Form** with a required **e-mail** field. This will be enough to get you started, so go ahead and press the **save & exit** button to finalize the form.

4. Next, we'll integrate MailChimp into your WordPress site by using the official MailChimp WordPress plugin. Log into your WordPress dashboard, navigate to **Plugins | Add New** and search for **MailChimp**.

5. Install the plugin labelled **MailChimp List Subscribe Form** by MailChimp and Crowd Favorite by clicking on the **Install Now** link located below the plugin name.

6. Connect your WordPress site with your MailChimp account through the plugin by navigating to **Settings | MailChimp Setup** and following the directions.

7. Select the **Signup Form** that you created in Step 2 from the drop-down selection and press the **Update List** button.

8. You'll be presented with several options, but for now, you can just uncheck the **Monkey Rewards** checkbox to remove the MailChimp branding and keep the remaining default settings as it is. Remember to press the **Update Subscribe Form Settings** button after you have made changes.

9. Embed the signup form into your site using the **MailChimp Widget** by navigating to **Appearance | Widgets** and dragging the widget wherever you want to display the form; you'll most likely want to consider your sidebar.

10. At this point, you should be able to see your newsletter subscription form on your website. Feel free to complete a test submission by filling out all the fields and pressing the **Subscribe** button. It should trigger a **double opt-in** notice, which means you will receive an e-mail that will require you to confirm the subscription.

11. Now, publish a test post titled **Matt Mullenweg** by navigating to **Posts | Add New**. You can write anything in the content area as long as it contains the word **Mullenweg**, as well. This will come in handy for Part 2.

 For further basic MailChimp training, be sure to register for a free webinar at `http://mailchimp.com/support/online-training/`. Also, be sure to check out their online resources at `http://mailchimp.com/resources/`.

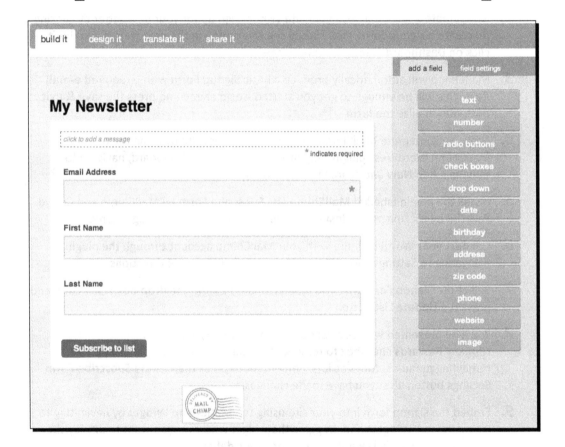

Part 2—creating a keyword-specific RSS feed

Moving on to the second portion of this activity, a custom RSS feed that is based on a keyword. We'll accomplish this with the help of Yahoo! Pipes, so you will need to register for a free Yahoo! account, if you don't already have a Google or Facebook account.

1. Log onto `http://pipes.yahoo.com/` and click on the prominent **Create a pipe** link located on the top navigation.

2. Drag the **Fetch Feed** module on the left window pane under the **Sources** header to workspace, which is the big, light-blue space located to the right. In the empty field, enter the name of your website's main RSS feed (`http://www.yourdomain.com/feed/`).

3. Click on the **Operators** header to reveal the **Filter** module. Drag the **Filter** module to the workspace. This will reveal a GUI for some basic `if-then` programming options.

4. Above the fields, make the following selections so that it reads **Permit** items that match any of the following.

5. In the left field of this module, select **item.description** from the drop-down selection.

6. Keep the default **Contains** option for the middle drop-down selection.

7. The right field is not a drop-down selection but rather a field for a specific value. In this case, the value is your keyword, so enter `Mullenweg` in this field.

8. Repeat Steps 4 through 6 by clicking on the **+Rules** button of the **Feed Fetch** module. However, select the **item.title** from the drop-down selection of the left field for this new rule.

9. Create a new rule that will ignore any content published prior to the date you've created this pipe, by selecting **item.pubDate** from the left field, selecting **is after** from the middle field and entering today's date in MM/DD/YYYY format in the right field (example: `10/11/2011` for October 10, 2011).

10. In your workspace, there should be a pipe connector represented by a circle centered above and/or below each pipe module. This is a where you can connect one module to another using a pipe. Connect your **Fetch Feed** module to the **Filter** module by click-holding on the bottom of the **Fetch Feed** module and then drawing (dragging) the pipe to the top of the **Filter** module.

11. Next, connect the **Filter** module to the **Pipe Output** module by click-holding on the bottom **Filter** pipe connector and drawing a pipe that leads to the **Pipe Output** connector.

12. You should now be able to view the output below the workspace in the gray area labelled **Debugger**. The output should display the test post from Step 11 of Part 1. You may need to press the **Refresh** link in the **Debugger** to view your content.

13. Click on the **Save** button located toward the top-left of your window and give it an appropriate name like `Mullenweg`.

14. To get the URL for this custom RSS feed, which you will use as material for your Mullenweg newsletter, click on the **Back To My Pipes** near the top to list your Yahoo! pipe. Click on the **Publish** link by hovering over your pipe to produce a publicly accessible RSS feed for this data.

15. Click on the orange RSS icon labelled **Get as RSS** to get the link to this feed and copy it somewhere, as you will need it for your MailChimp campaign.

 For detailed information on RSS-based e-mails, visit `http://mailchimp.com/features/rss-to-email/`.

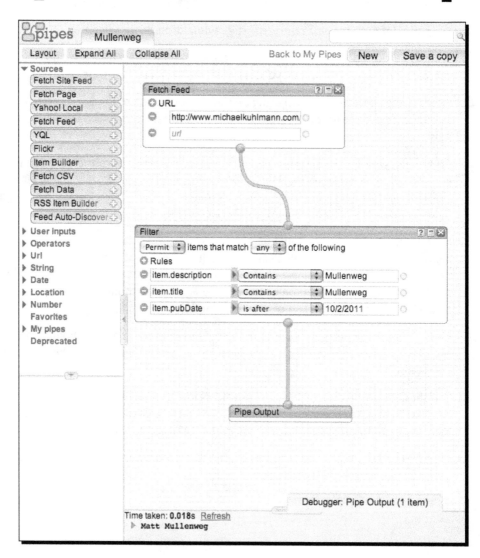

Part 3—creating an automated newsletter campaign

In this last part of the tutorial, you will create a newsletter campaign that uses the custom RSS feed from Part 2 as newsletter material for your Mullenweg subscribers.

1. In your MailChimp dashboard, navigate to **Campaigns** in the top navigation.

2. Click on the large **create campaign** button and select **RSS-driven campaign**.

3. In the **RSS feed URL** field, paste the RSS feed link from Step 15 of Part 2 and select the appropriate mailing frequency for your Mullenweg newsletter campaign.

4. Click on **Next** to select the subscriber list that is associated with the subscriber form that you've created in Step 2 of Part 1. Do not send anything yet. Instead, click on **Next**.

5. Under the **Campaign Info**, give your newsletter campaign an appropriate name that corresponds to your newsletter.

6. Click on **Next** again to move on to the design portion of this campaign and select the **basic (500px)** e-mail template for your newsletter. Once you have made the selection, you'll be able to preview the e-mail with some sample copy.

7. To replace the sample copy with your custom RSS feed data, you will need to hover over the sample copy and click on the **edit** button to launch a text editor. Then, click on the **source** button to edit the html source code.

8. Replace everything with the following code:

   ```
   *|RSS:POSTS_HTML|*
   ```

9. Continue by clicking on **Next** and skip the plain text e-mail delivery options by clicking on **Next** again.

10. In the final step of the MailChimp newsletter campaign setup, you can send a test e-mail newsletter to yourself by clicking on the **send a test** link located at the bottom of the page. Alternatively, you can also start your automated newsletter mailing campaign by clicking on the **start RSS campaign** button:

 You will want to test everything to ensure proper delivery before going live. You may also want to revisit your **MailChimp e-mail** template through some image and CSS edits to match your branding. To download the e-mail template used in this example, visit `http://socialmediaforwp.com/downloads/mailchimp-email-template/`.

What just happened?

In the activity, we provided the readers with a newsletter that was automatically sent to them on a regular basis, using a double opt-in e-mailing method. The content for this newsletter was based on a RSS feed that was filtered by a keyword.

First, we created a place on your WordPress site where visitors could input their e-mail addresses to receive your newsletter, using a third-party ESP. The e-mail newsletter content was created using another third-party service that enabled you to pull certain RSS feeds and filter the content. A campaign was then initiated to automate the e-mail newsletter service.

Utilizing MailChimp and Yahoo! Pipes

There are several ESPs and RSS aggregator services online, but why did we use MailChimp and Yahoo! Pipes? The answer is simple: they are both reputable services that are not prone to shutting down like most other free services. Additionally, MailChimp has sponsored many WordCamps to empower the WordPress community with innovative e-mailing capabilities. Yahoo! Pipes, on the other hand, lets you visually create the flow of information, which means that you don't need to be a skilled programmer; you merely need to determine the source and presentation of the data and Pipes does the rest. Many RSS aggregators only mash feeds together, but they won't let you filter data by keywords, dates, or other criteria. Yahoo! Pipes fills that void by providing the extra flexibility. Both services excel at simplifying processes that would otherwise be unbearable.

Partnering and building sponsorship opportunities

Newsletters by themselves can sometimes still be boring pieces of data that hit your inbox on a regular basis. The key to driving more interest in your site is through **content segmentation**—splitting your content into multiple channels. It's not that they don't want to receive your news; they just don't want to receive all of it. Committing to a barrage of constant e-mails is no easy feat, especially if your only options are to subscribe or not to subscribe. You need to provide more gateways to make your content more accessible such as using social media sharing buttons, as you'll read in Chapter 7, so that your readers will want to share it with like-minded people.

On the flipside, you will want to create automated e-mail campaigns like this, because it opens up the door to partnering and sponsorship opportunities. For example, you could embed ads in your newsletters or post links to your partners. Using Yahoo! Pipes, you're also able to fetch your partners' or sponsors' RSS feeds, if you don't have the resources to produce content yourself.

Exploring more applications to this tutorial

The three-part tutorial extends itself to more areas than an automated newsletter. The first part really introduced you to **lead generation**—the process in which you collect information from prospective customers on whether they are interested in your content. MailChimp even rates your subscribers, based on how they interact with your e-mails and signup forms. The ability to tie this functionality into WordPress only empowers your site to grow, because you can use the same process for white papers or other valuable information that you'd like to exchange for site visitor information. The clearer the picture you can paint of your visitors, the better you'll be able to produce content that they will want to talk about and share with others.

Part 2 of the tutorial allowed you to peek into the concept of **content aggregation**, meaning that you're gathering website material for your own site that has already been published elsewhere. MailChimp does not require you to use a customized RSS feed like you learned in the activity. In fact, you can use WordPress category feeds to create your newsletter or whatever you want to send out. Going through the process and fine-tuning the content, however, has taught you to look at it in a different light.

Pop quiz – understanding key terms and key concepts

1. An ESP allows you to connect RSS feeds together.

    a. True

    b. False

2. You can only use one RSS feed source at a time when building a Yahoo! Pipe.

    a. True

    b. False

3. Ping-O-Matic allows you to collect subscriber information for mailing campaigns.

    a. True

    b. False

4. The process in which you collect information from prospective customers on whether they are interested in your content is called lead generation.

    a. True

    b. False

5. You can use Yahoo! Pipes to customize any and all of your WordPress RSS feeds.

    a. True

    b. False

Have a go hero

You can think about your WordPress site as just a blog or simple content management system, but what if it could evoke a feeling of unity and belonging? What if your content was powerful enough for your visitors to keep coming back to it and what if you could provide them with enough content channels for them to stay engaged? Your site could change the way a soccer league stays in contact, or how a local restaurant can retain its customers with a food menu newsletter. It all has to do with the flow of data and what you do with it to enable your site visitors, users, and followers to connect with one another.

Summary

This chapter introduced you to several concepts and ideas that will help you make the most of your site, without getting too heavy on customizing WordPress itself.

Specifically, we covered the following:

- Social media can have historical impacts as long as it is about building a meaningful dialog with your audience
- WordPress has three powerful core functions that help you promote social sharing
- Segmenting your content is key to lead generation and content aggregation.
- Third-party services such as MailChimp and Yahoo! Pipes can be tremendously helpful in lead generation and content aggregation
- You don't need to be a skilled programmer with a completely customized WordPress theme to get more interaction out of your site
- We also discussed how building e-mail campaigns can lend themselves to partnering and sponsorship opportunities, which will undoubtedly help you with your return on investment

Now that we've learned about the basic aspect of social media, we're ready to get our hands dirty with two big plugins called BuddyPress and WP Symposium, which are commonly referred to as *Facebook in a box*.

2
Building the Social Network: BuddyPress and WP Symposium

It took Mark Zuckerberg about one month to build the first iteration of Facebook. It'll take you only five minutes to build it yourself. Here's the drawback—it'll be just as easy for others, too. Competition is inevitable.

In the first chapter, we covered the importance of your site content and how you can funnel and deliver your content to your audience for easier access. Now, we'll go over some ideas on how you can drive social interactions using plugins, which will greatly extend your WordPress site. Specifically, we'll learn the following:

- Preparations for rolling out your social media layer
- Top ten plugins that will help you with BuddyPress development
- Adding game-like capabilities to help you engage your site members
- How to adapt and convert site visitors into site members
- Benefits of using different social networks to connect to your site
- How user-generated content can have a tremendous impact on your site

So let's get started...

Before you enable the social layer

As tempting as it may seem, going into your WordPress site and activating **BuddyPress (BP)** and **WP Symposium (WPS)** simultaneously is the last thing you want to do. It would be the equivalent of wearing a helmet, while you're driving a car around the block. Twice the same functionality does not translate into a better experience. Since the former is the more established plugin, the activities in this chapter, will focus on BuddyPress. Before you get started, however, there are a few things you'll want to consider, outlined as follows.

Take a measured approach to your feature rollout

There is a great amount of noise you have to consider before rolling out a site that features status updates, private messaging, or group discussions. Text messages, tweets, Facebook updates, incoming e-mails, and other disruptive stimuli are already vying for your visitors' attention. Thus limiting the window of opportunity for them to engage with each other. Even with the amount of social components available to you, you're more likely to fatigue your users, if you unleash all of them at once. Chances are that you are more excited about these site additions than your users. The proper term for this occurrence is **attention economics**, which assumes site visitors will navigate away from your site, if it takes them too long to navigate within your site to find what they're looking for. As mentioned in the previous chapter, keep your site simple at first and activate these components after your visitors have outgrown your other features. The last thing they want to do is register for yet another site, set up another group of friends, manage another account, and attempt to navigate around another Facebook clone.

Make your passion your niche market

It's exciting to discover there's open source software available on the web, which allows you to build social applications like Facebook, Twitter, and YouTube. However, building existing social applications in WordPress doesn't provide much incentive for your user. In order to stay relevant and preserve exclusivity, you have to find a niche market that you're thoroughly passionate about. If you're an ardent television watcher and care about music, you may want to create a site focused on American Idol, for example, since you're already invested in it. Nothing is more challenging than building a site around a topic you don't find stimulating.

Set aside time

If you've already found your niche market and you're ready to start a meaningful dialog with your users, then you've already completed half the work. The other half will come in the form of clocking in more work hours than you'll anticipate. Adding a social layer to your WordPress site means more storage, more bandwidth allocation, more operational management, and generally, more accountability on your part. It means that you will most likely be a point of contact for troubleshooting, should a user encounter a pressing issue with his or her account. You are going to be the wheels and axles for your social media vehicle, meaning you need to demonstrate the competency of your users' needs. If you have doubts about time allocation or commitment, see if you can distribute some tasks and roles to people who may be interested in helping you, before you release your new features.

 A BuddyPress-powered site allows for easy partnerships. If you feel overwhelmed, see if you can get somebody involved who is equally invested in your interests. In exchange, you can provide free advertising through a marketing campaign, which you've learned about in *Chapter 1, Share it the Easy Way*.

Top 10 plugins to supplement your BuddyPress site

BuddyPress is a plugin that enables a suite of components for people to interact with each other on your site. Out of the box, it ships with the following features:

♦   activity streams

♦   extended profiles

♦   friend connections

♦   private messaging

♦   extensible groups

♦   discussion forums

♦   WordPress blogging

This sounds dandy until you enable them, which leads to an initial user interest that may increase your site traffic. But what may also happen is that your site will start to lose steam in the adoption process with the onslaught of new features, and your traffic will decrease, following the shape of the bell curve or standard deviation. For example, let's imagine you relaunch your site with BuddyPress. Over a one-month period, you'll see traffic steadily rise. You may get one new registered member per day, which will increase to four members per day in the following week, three members per day in the third week, and two members per day in the last week. Some members may never revisit your site again and only a portion will continue to log into your site.

The culprit of this lacklustre growth is typically feature overload, which might frustrate your users as they're presented with an array of tools that they don't know how to use. Luckily, there are several plugins to help your traffic follow the shape of the exponential growth curve instead:

- **Welcome Pack**: It's a tall order to expect new site visitors to know how to interact with each other upon the first few visits. This plugin allows you to redirect new users to a **Start** page, where you can introduce your site features and/or activities. Learn more at http://wordpress.org/extend/plugins/welcome-pack/.

- **Achievements for BuddyPress**: This plugin dabbles with the concept of **gamification**—the process of adding gaming components to engage your audience, in the form of badges and points that users can earn by unlocking *Achievements* through social interactions on your site similar to FourSquare's gaming features. Learn more at http://wordpress.org/extend/plugins/achievements/.

- **BP Labs**: Although this BuddyPress extension states that it's in perpetual beta with its Labs moniker, you will find extensive use out of it, because it uses Automattic's Akismet technology to get rid of spam comments in your activity stream. Learn more at http://wordpress.org/extend/plugins/bp-labs/.

- **WP-FB-AutoConnect**: Whether you love or loathe it, Facebook boasts upwards of 800 million active users. Using this plugin, you'll be able to make them BuddyPress (and WordPress) users with a Facebook sign in button, bypassing the typical registration process and, thereby, lowering the barrier of entry to your site. Learn more at http://wordpress.org/extend/plugins/wp-fb-autoconnect/.

- **Buddypress Template Pack**: Creating your own BuddyPress theme can be very time consuming, even if it is just a child theme of the parent BP Default theme. Activating this plugin lets you keep your current site theme and also sets up the BP modules for you, so you can spend more time managing rather than coding it. Learn more at http://wordpress.org/extend/plugins/bp-template-pack/.

- **HeadSpace2 SEO**: Contrary to its title, this not only comes in handy as far as search engine optimizing, but it also allows you to easily embed page-specific JavaScript and CSS without touching a line of code in your function.PHP file. Learn more at http://wordpress.org/extend/plugins/headspace2/.

- **WP Super Popup**: There will come a time when you want to promote something on your site. This plugin is a simple and effective solution to accomplish that task, using a prominent pop up with a WYSIWYG editor. Learn more at http://wordpress.org/extend/plugins/wordpress-popup/.

- **XCloner - Backup and Restore**: This is a plugin that backs up your entire site including all tables in your MySQL database as well as non-WordPress specific directories and files. It also lets you automate scheduled backups and send backups to Amazon's S3 cloud storage, providing you with the perfect backup plan. Learn more at http://wordpress.org/extend/plugins/xcloner-backup-and-restore/.

- **W3 Total Cache**: BuddyPress can be a heavy burden on your server, especially when site traffic starts to pick up. Using this caching plugin alleviates some of that server load and also speeds up your site, making for a better **User Experience (UX)**. Learn more at `http://wordpress.org/extend/plugins/w3-total-cache/`.

- **Gravity Forms**: This premium plugin allows you to create forms, using a drag-and-drop interface. You can use various input types including post fields such as the title, excerpt, tag, and category to experiment with **User-Generated Content (UGC)**. Learn more at `http://www.gravityforms.com/`.

Gravity Forms

Once in a while, a plugin comes along that will significantly improve your productivity, because of an intelligible user interface. **Gravity Forms** is one of those plugins. Although you can mimic some of its functionality with free alternatives like **Contact Form 7** and **TDO Mini Forms**, they do not come close when it comes to ease of use. Even worse, sometimes the free plugins aren't supported at all. **Gravity Forms** is reputable and feature-rich, in comparison, making it a quick turnaround solution for advanced form building. Purchasing a license for this plugin also includes support and feature requests.

The first half of plugins listed above are BuddyPress-specific. In fact, the first three are developed by BuddyPress core developer Paul Gibbs, so you won't have to worry too much about whether it will be abandoned down the road or leave any loopholes for hackers. While the second half of the listed plugins are not dependent on BuddyPress, they are essential to easing your workflow for site development and maintenance.

Activating BuddyPress plugins

Activating any or all of the BuddyPress plugins listed above is as simple as activating normal WordPress plugins.

1. First, we will install BuddyPress. Navigate to **Plugins | Add New**, search for **BuddyPress**, click on the **Install Now** link located under the plugin name, proceed with your FTP connection and click on the **Activate Plugin** link. Follow the remaining steps, using the BuddyPress installation wizard that should take you through a process where you can select which social media components you want to enable, as illustrated in the following screenshot (More detailed instructions can be found at `http://codex.buddypress.org/getting-started/setting-up-a-new-installation/`).

2. To install any supplemental plugins, follow Step 1 again and search for the other plugins that you'd like to activate. Starting out, you will most likely only need to activate the **BuddyPress Template Pack** plugin, if you want to keep the appearance of your current site.

3. To configure your plugins, you'll usually be able to access those options under **Settings**. As **BuddyPress** is building a whole social layer on top of WordPress, it gets its own dedicated section under **Settings**:

What just happened?

You have just broken ground on your BuddyPress site. It isn't ready for prime time yet, as visitors to your site will undoubtedly try to take a peek at your barren **Activity Stream** or **Members** section, which will most likely only be populated by you, at this point. Logged-in users like yourself will also see a new admin bar spanning across the top of your page. It includes links to view your activity, profile, messages, friends, groups, and account settings.

The Default BuddyPress theme

If you're working off a fresh WordPress installation and only have the BuddyPress plugin activated, you'll see the official BuddyPress default theme (**DTheme**) automatically activated. It is reminiscent of an older Facebook layout with its tabbed sections and minimal design. Changing the background and header of this theme can be easily accomplished with the theme's built-in **User-Interface (UI)**. By and large, you can use the **DTheme** for an intranet or small niche site where branding and design isn't a priority, as the theme only offers a few styling options. Luckily, changing a BuddyPress theme is as easy as changing a WordPress theme. Following are a few helpful links to get you further acquainted with the plugin:

- What you should know: Learn more at `http://codex.buddypress.org/getting-started/what-you-should-know/`
- Installing a compatible theme: learn more at `http://codex.buddypress.org/extending-buddypress/installing-a-bp-compatible-theme/`
- Configuring components: Learn more at `http://codex.buddypress.org/getting-started/configure-buddypress-components/configuring-buddypress-components-for-bp-1-2/`
- Building a child theme: Learn more at `http://codex.buddypress.org/theme-development/building-a-buddypress-child-theme/`
- Support—How to and troubleshooting: Learn more at `http://buddypress.org/community/groups/how-to-and-troubleshooting/forum/`

The Facebook connection

Although there are many good Facebook plugins available on the WordPress repository, the impetus for creating a BP-powered site is usually data liberation, the freedom to own your data and migrate it wherever you like. It's not necessarily frowned upon to integrate the **Facebook Tab Manager** plugin, for example, but it's also not everyone's cup of tea to hand over that data and have their account tethered to Facebook. The measured approach is to consider asking your members if they would like their site data to appear on Facebook, as well.

Prepare for a work in progress

Social networks are ubiquitous. To effectively grow your site and stay competitive, you will have to dedicate a lot of resources. It may come in the form of putting in the extra hour to ask your members for site feedback, or it may come in the form of spending money on a premium plugin or service. It also means the BuddyPress portion of your site will undergo continuous change over the months to better accommodate your users, as they acclimate to the added features:

Pop quiz – buddyPress Basics

1. You can set up your BP-powered site in five minutes.

    a. True

    b. False

2. The broader you keep your site, the more people you'll attract.

    a. True

    b. False

3. All WordPress and BuddyPress plugins are free.

    a. True

    b. False

4. Gamification is the process of adding gaming components to engage your audience.

    a. True

    b. False

5. Integrating a Facebook with WordPress is considered bad practice.

    a. True

    b. False

Easing your users into BuddyPress

Taking the path with the least amount of resistance roughly translates into disabling several BuddyPress components. There is a good chance you probably went through the BuddyPress installation wizard and enabled every single component. You may have even gone the extra step to install bbPress for forum integration, but what we'll do now is curb some of that functionality in favor of polishing one component—**Extended Profiles**, the extra tidbits of information users fill out about themselves like age, location, and so forth.

Time for action – how to convert site visitors to site members

Yes, you can just display a prominent **Register Now** button somewhere on your website, but for a small, fledgling site that's just starting out, you want to be more proactive about getting new site visitors to convert to site members. We'll complete this three-part activity by first connecting your WordPress site with Facebook, welcoming your new site members and then rewarding them with points.

Part 1—connecting your WordPress site with Facebook

1. Install and activate the following plugins from the aforementioned top 10 list: **WP-FB-AutoConnect**, **Welcome Pack**, **Achievement for BuddyPress** and **WP Super Popup**. We'll only use **FB-AutoConnect** for this part of the activity.

2. Log into your Facebook account and go to `https://developers.facebook.com/apps`.

3. In the upper-right corner, click on the **Create New App** button to create the application, which will connect WordPress with Facebook.

4. In the **Create New App** pop-up window, enter the **App Display Name**, which can be the name of your website, as that is what users will see upon logging into your WordPress site using their Facebook account, as shown in the following screenshot:

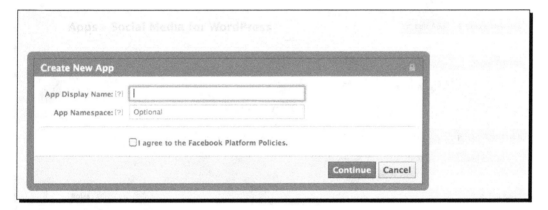

5. Enter the **App Namespace**, which can be the same name as the **App Display Name**, provided that it is at least seven characters long and only contains lowercase letters, dashes, and underscores.

6. Check off the **Facebook Platform Policies** and press the **Continue** button and proceed with the **Security Check**. You should now see the basic settings of your new app, but don't close the browser window just yet, as you'll need to access some information for the **WP-FB-AutoConnect** plugin.

7. Scroll down the section labeled **Select how your app integrates with Facebook**, check off **Website** and enter the full web address (URL) of your WordPress site. See the following screenshot for how your Facebook application page should look:

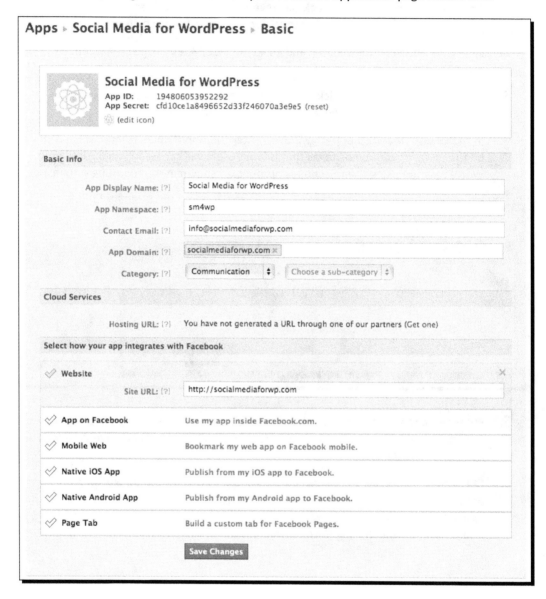

8. Next, navigate to your WordPress Dashboard and go to **WP-FB AutoConn** under **Settings**. You can skip past the directions and fill out the two pieces of information requested below— the **API Key** and the **API Secret**, as shown in the following screenshot:

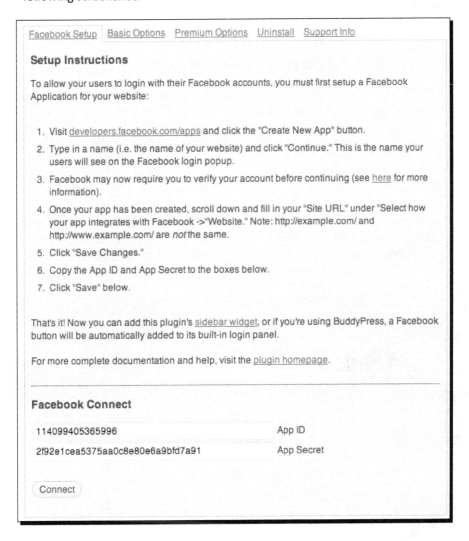

9. Using the open browser window from Step 6, this information can be found in your Facebook App under **Basic** in the **Settings** section. The **API Key** requested by the plugin is labeled **App ID** and the **API Secret** is labeled **App Secret**. If you accidentally closed the window from Step 6, you can still access this information by revisiting `https://developers.facebook.com/apps`. Your new app should be the first one listed under **Recently Viewed** in the left sidebar.

10. Press the **Connect** button to connect WordPress with Facebook.

11. Under the **Options** section of the plugin, check off **Use Facebook profile pictures as avatars** and press the **Save** button. If you log out of WordPress, you should now be able to log into your site's homepage, using the blue **Login with Facebook** button, if you're running the BuddyPress default theme.

Part 2—greeting your new visitors with a warm welcome

1. First, create your welcome page in WordPress by navigating to **Add New** under **Pages** and give it a title like **Welcome**.

2. In the content field, you can write or list a few perks about your site, since this is what new users will see upon the first login, as shown in the example. If you can't think of anything, that's okay. For now, just write something along the lines of You can unlock Achievements through several ways and link it to your **Achievements** page, which will be located at http://www.yourdomain.tld/achievements/ (we'll cover this in Part 3). Don't forget to press the **Publish** button to make this page accessible. You may also want to disable **trackbacks** and **comments**. (Note: You can download the code for the example page shown here at http://socialmediaforwp.com/downloads/welcome-page-template/).

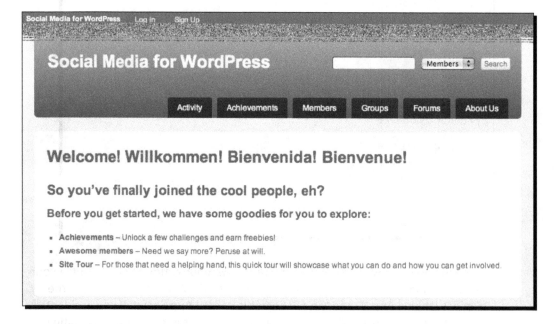

3. Next, navigate to **Welcome Pack** under **Settings**.

4. Enable the **Start Page** and **Welcome Message** by pressing the **On** buttons and click on the **Save Changes** button, which should display the **Start Page** and **Welcome Message** tabs.

5. Click on the **Start Page** tab, enter the URL to your **Welcome** page from Step 1 and press the **Save Changes** button, as shown in the following screenshot:

6. Click on the **Welcome Message** tab and write the same copy from Step 1; you can get more original if you want, but this will work for now. See the following screenshot for an example. New site visitors will see a notification alert that will link to this **Message** upon the first time logging in. So be sure to keep the subject line descriptive, as you'll also receive an e-mailed copy of the same message:

7. Navigate to **Achievements** under **BuddyPress** and click on the **Achievements Directory** link. If you see a floating warning message in your dashboard that states **The following active BuddyPress Components do not have associated WordPress Pages: Achievements. Repair**, it means that you will have to create this **Achievements Directory** page first.

8. To create the **Achievements Directory** page, go to **Add New** under **Pages**, give it a title of **Achievements** (make sure the slug remains **Achievements**) and **Publish** your page. This will only be a placeholder for the automatically generated **Achievements** page, so any content you write into the content field will not be displayed. Then, go back to **Achievements** under **BuddyPress**, map the **Achievements** page from the drop-down menu with the **Achievements** option and press the **Save Changes** button, as shown in the following screenshot. Your **Achievements** page should now be accessible at `http://www.yourdomain.tld/achievements/`:

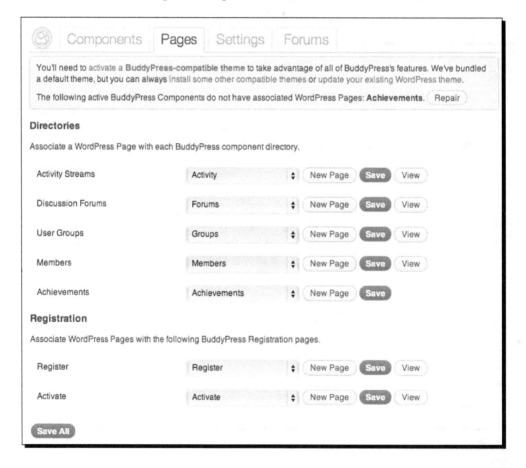

9. Navigate to your **Achievements** page and press the **Create an Achievement** button.

10. In the **Action** section, select **Event** for the **Type** and choose **User updates their profile** from the **Event** drop-down selection. Keep the default number for **When the event occurs this many times**, as **1**.

11. You can assign any name for the **Name** field in the **Info** section, but be sure to enter a brief description as how to unlock this **Achievement**. Write something like Update your profile to unlock this Achievement.

12. You can enter any numeric value for the points, but try to follow a structure. You can assign points in single increments (1, 2, 3, 4) or multiples of 5 (5, 10, 15, 20), for example but now try **5** points, as shown in the following screenshot:

13. In the **Advanced Settings** section, be sure to check **Active** and then press the **Create Achievement** button to save all your changes. You may be redirected to a page where you can choose a graphic to represent this **Achievement**. Pick one as you can always go back later and change that, as well.

Part 3—providing your new site visitor with incentives

1. Navigate to **Super Popup** and check **Popup enabled** for the **Status**.

2. The mobile option really depends on your preference, so we'll keep the default value, which is **No**; popups are notoriously difficult to close on small devices.

3. Keep the **Back** link on the footer unchecked and select **Show the popup only for the following paths** for the Paths **inclusion/exclusion** option.

4. In the big text field for this option, enter the URL to your **Achievements** page from Step 8 of Part 2, as illustrated in the following screenshot:

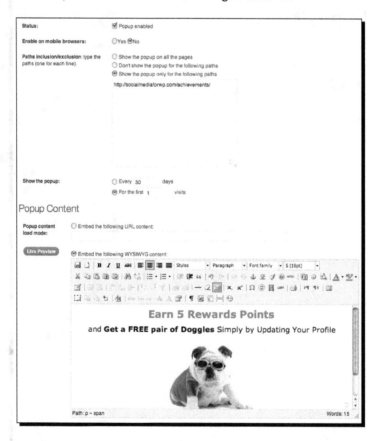

5. For the **Show the popup** option, select and enter **For the first 1 visits** to display this popup only once.

6. Give your new users a reason for them to update their profile in the **Popup Content** section by selecting the **Embed the following WYSIWYG content** option. You can write something like `Earn 5 Rewards Points Simply by Updating Your Profile!` If you have free giveaways, you can write something like `Earn 5 Rewards Points and Get a FREE Pair of Doggles Simply by Updating Your Profile!` Try to give your call-to-action some pizzazz by playing around with the formatting. The following example illustrates the popup with some color and size formatting along with a funny graphic of a dog sporting doggles that's sure to spawn some reactions.

7. You can edit the **Visual Effects Settings** to suit your taste, but we'll keep everything at their default values for now. Finally, be sure to press the **Save Changes** button:

What just happened?

You created a small Facebook application that allowed you to connect your WordPress site with Facebook. The WP-FB auto-connect plugin then allowed new visitors to log into your site, using their Facebook credentials. This was done to tap into the pool of 800-plus million Facebook users who could be prospective site members. It also simplified the registration process, since new visitors didn't have to provide any new information to access your site, thereby lowering the barrier of entry.

In Step 2, you created a **Welcome** Page to ease your users to your site, so they could familiarize themselves a bit more with your content. Here, you also linked to your **Achievements** page, which we created in Step 3, to pique their interest. The **Achievements** page was really a two-fold solution to the following questions: how do you engage your audience, and what's in it for them? Using a pop-up window, you answered that question by providing them with a numerical incentive in the form of five rewards points and possibly a freebie.

Use your own voice

In this activity, you used sample copy to complete all the steps. However, you should always use your own voice when you write. If you usually don't use many apostrophes, or usually sound incredibly cheery, revisit those areas and make it sound more like you. Your visitors will know something is off-key, if the tone of your content sounds unusual. It may even sound too much like a sales pitch, so do not let yourself fall into this trap. If your typical writing style drips with sarcasm, you should be equally sarcastic in your welcome page, welcome e-mail, and achievements pop-up.

Don't overwhelm your new site members

You will be tempted to mention everything under the sun when it comes to your welcome page. Be engaging but keep it short and sweet, as your new members do not need a full-fledged site tour. If you feel that they do, you can always highlight the tour in a bullet item and link to a separate page replete with videos, screenshots, and testimonials. The welcome page is merely there to give your new site members a warm greeting, while pointing out your site's best features. Similarly, do not go crazy with your popups.

Profiling your site members

What you've just covered in this activity is the concept of progressive profiling. You gave your visitors some points (or even a freebie) and, in exchange, they provided you with personal details about themselves through Extended Profiles. If you repeat this process with more points or rewards, in exchange for more information, you will eventually be able to draw a full picture of your users. This will help you gain a better understanding of their interests, so you can tweak your site appropriately with more meaningful content, which will drive more conversations. Remember, the key to building a useful profile for a user depends on the content of your site. For example, if you're building a social network on exotic sports cars, you should probably create profile fields that relate to cars, not politics or religion.

Pop quiz – audience engagement

1. You need to use WP-FB Autoconnect to take advantage of the Achievements page.

    a. True

    b. False

2. Try to reward your visitors with multiple popups, as they need to be engaged.

    a. True

    b. False

3. Providing as much information as you can fit into your Welcome Page is detrimental to the success of the initial visit for a new site user.

    a. True

    b. False

4. You can use any point system when your create Achievements.

    a. True

    b. False

5. Progressive profiling means that you'll learn more information about your site visitors every time they log in.

    a. True

    b. False

Gamification: The art of user-generated content

When it comes to your BuddyPress-powered site, you want to make it fun like a game. Posting updates, earning points, and the like should be fun, not a chore. In the previous activity, you provided a user with an incentive to complete an action, which resulted in a profile data transaction that benefitted you as the site owner. Taking this a step further, you can also tie this in with **User-Generated Content (UGC)** by allowing your members to post content to your site without much work on your part. Best of all, the more UGC that's produced, the more your site will become a social media vehicle for your niche.

Time for action – how to get your users to create original content for you

Increasing your conversion rate for site visitors to site members can be as easy as providing another outlet for your users to interact with your site. If visitors see a flurry of activity on your site through status updates, post publications, comments, or any other form, they will be more likely to become an active member than if you did not support any of those options.

Now, we'll get more creative by allowing your site members to produce content for you, using the **Gravity Forms** plugin and **AddThis** service, which is a free third-party social bookmarking service that allows you to share content. For this two-part activity, we'll let your users create reviews and ratings, which they will be able to share.

Part 1—create a post content form with ratings

1. Navigate to **Categories** under **Posts** and create a new category with a **Name** and **Slug** of **Reviews**.

2. If you haven't purchased **Gravity Forms**, log on to http://www.gravityforms.com. You can purchase the personal license for this activity, but you'll get more out of the developer version with its multiple add-ons such as MailChimp and PayPal integration. Purchase, install, and activate the plugin.

3. Next, navigate to **New Form** under **Forms** and click on **Post Fields** under **Add Fields** located to the right.

4. Click on the **Title** button to add the post title field, which will populate your form with the **Post Title**. In the **Post Title** field, you click on the **Edit** button to reveal more options.

5. Enter **Product or Service** for the **Field Label** option, as this will tell your users that this field is intended for a particular product or service name.

6. Select **Published** under the **Post Status** drop-down selection, so that the submitted content will be automatically posted instead of being queued up for admin review.

7. Select an appropriate post author for the **Default Post Author** in the drop-down selection. If you do not have one or don't want to use your admin account, you can always create a new user by navigating to **Add New** under **Users** in the main dashboard navigation to the left. Also, check logged in user as author so that the product or service review is attributed to your site member, as this will be used instead of the **Default Post Author**, which will only be used for non-registered users.

8. Select **Reviews** from the **Post Category** drop-down selection, which is the category you created in Step 1.

9. Select the **Required** field under **Rules**, so that site visitors will know what product or service is being reviewed. Save your progress for now by clicking on the **Save Form** button and continue editing your form.

10. Click on the **Body** button under the **Post Fields** options to the right to add the post content for your form. This will be the actual review (that is, post content) of the product or service.

11. Click on the **Edit** link for this form field and make the same selections for this field as you did for the **Post Title** field (repeat Steps 7 to 11).

12. Click on the **Category** button under the **Post Fields** options to the right to add the post category for this review and click on the **Edit** button.

13. Choose **Reviews** from the **Select Categories** option under **Categories**, so that your submitted form will be automatically categorized. Under the **Advanced** tab, select **Admin Only** for the **Visibility**, as you don't want your site users to see this.

14. Click on the **Tags** button under the **Post Fields** option to the right, which we'll use as our ratings scheme, and click on the **Edit** link so that you can change the **Field Label** to **Rating**.

15. Select **Multiple Choice** under the **Field Type** and enter the five choices in the following order, starting from the top—**Excellent**, **Very Good**, **Average**, **Fair**, **Poor** (click on the plus icon to add more choices when completing this step). Be sure to mark **Required** under **Rules**, since this is what people consider first for reviews. The finished form should look like the following screenshot.

16. Save and exit the form for now. You can also download this form to use as a template at `http://socialmediaforwp.com/downloads/ugc-gform/`:

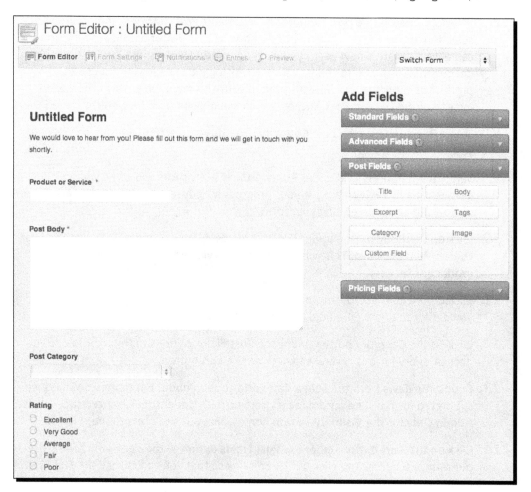

Using TDO Mini Forms instead of Gravity Forms

Part 1 can be replicated using a free plugin called **TDO Mini Forms**. The biggest disadvantages of using this alternative is that its developer no longer works or supports it. TDO Mini Forms can be extremely risky, if you encounter a critical error that affects your site, as it will be up to you or another developer to troubleshoot it. Other disadvantages include ease of use and extensibility, compared to **Gravity Forms**, which is simplistic in its nature and also supports PayPal payments and custom registration forms for WordPress and BuddyPress members. Nevertheless, if you feel TDO Mini Forms will suffice for you, you can follow the activity at `http://socialmediaforwp.com/activitys/tdo-mini-forms`

What just happened?

To get site members to produce content for you, they needed to access a page on your site where they could easily submit their content and have it automatically posted, which was achieved through the use of **Gravity Forms**. **Gravity Forms** enabled you to create a user submission form, which utilized the post title, content, category, and tag fields.

Time for action – how to enable users to share your content

By now, sharing content using social media icons is common practice. If you visit any publishing site, you will see multiple buttons that make it easier for the reader to share a story. In this case, you're going to enable authors to share their content more easily. The last thing people want to do is click on the browser's address bar, copy the link, start up a new browser session, paste the link somewhere and then send it off to a friend. It's not what they're used to, so let's provide this same functionality found on many other sites to simplify this process.

Part 2—simplifying the process of sharing user reviews

1. Since BuddyPress doesn't ship with automatic sharing capabilities through Facebook, Twitter, or any other social network out of the box, we'll use AddThis instead. If you don't have a Facebook, Twitter, Google, or Open ID account, register for a free AddThis account at `http://www.addthis.com`, by clicking on the **Join Now** link in the top right corner.

2. By default, AddThis displays four social media icons of 11 default services, using the most recently used destinations. However, to customize these icons and the URL they should point to, we'll have to modify the code by using the following snippet, which calls for the Facebook, Twitter, MySpace, and e-mail icons.

```
<div class="addthis_toolbox addthis_default_style addthis_32x32_
style" addthis:url="http://www.yourdomain.tld/?p={post_id}"
addthis:title="Read my latest review at">
<a class="addthis_button_facebook"></a>
<a class="addthis_button_twitter"></a>
<a class="addthis_button_myspace"></a>
<a class="addthis_button_email"></a>
</div>
<script type="text/javascript" src="http://s7.addthis.com/js/250/
addthis_widget.js">
</script>
```

3. More information on AddThis customization can be found at `https://www.addthis.com/help/client-api#rendering-preferred-services`

4. Back in your WordPress dashboard, return to the form you created in Part 1 by navigating to **Edit** Forms under **Forms**.

5. Hovering over the first form field, which will most likely read **Untitled Form** in bold, click on the **Edit** link and navigate to the **Confirmation** tab. Be sure to select the **Text** option for this form confirmation under the **Confirmation Message** option.

6. In the text field under the **Confirmation Message** option, write something like `Share this review using any of the services listed below` to preface the social media icons as illustrated in the following screenshot, which also shows how a tweet looks like if you press the **Twitter** icon.

7. Paste the code snippet from Step 2 below and be sure to select **Disable Auto-formatting** under the text field, as the code snippet contains JavaScript. You may also use inline CSS to further style any of the elements that will be displayed.

8. If you haven't labeled your form yet, you may do so now by clicking on the **Properties** tab of your form and changing the **Title** to **Review**. Be sure to press **Update Form** button below to save all your changes and finish your form.

9. Create a new page by navigating to **Add New** under **Pages**. Give your new page an appropriate title like **Review**.

10. To display your form on this page, click on the form icon, which will be the fifth icon from the left next to **Upload/Insert** below the page title field. If you're unsure about the icon, hover your mouse pointer over it to display the icon title, which should read **Add Gravity Form**.

11. Select your form (for example, **Review**) from the drop-down selection, uncheck all options, and click on the **Insert Form** button, which will produce a line of WordPress code also known as shortcode.

12. Uncheck **comments**, **trackbacks**, and **pingbacks** in the **Discussion** section, and **Publish** your page to reveal your **Review** section with social sharing options:

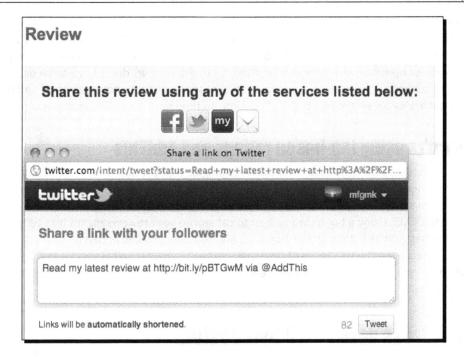

 You can take this activity a step further by integrating **Achievements** for BuddyPress. For example, you could add one more line of copy that reads **Earn 10 points if you share your review on your Activity stream** and create a new **Achievement** for this action.

What just happened?

Upon the posting of the content from Part 1, your users also needed to be able to share it through popular social networking sites such as Facebook and Twitter, which was accomplished using the **AddThis** service. You also modified the **AddThis** service to use only certain social networking services.

Why post reviews and ratings matter

Facemash, a hot-or-not-like rating site based on students' ID pictures, was Mark Zuckerberg's predecessor to Facebook. Although ethically and morally wrong within the university setting, he collected this personal information without prior consent from each individual. It became an overnight sensation logging 22,000 photo-views in its first four hours online, because the process of rating students' pictures was easy and engaging. Post reviews and ratings matter, because they represent Facemash in that they are just as easy to produce and consume, making them just as engaging. They also represent the success of Amazon's product ratings, as well as other sites utilizing consumer reviews.

First, they provide new and original content, which not only drives site traffic, but also helps with **Search Engine Optimization (SEO)**, since more relevant content gets indexed by search bots. Reviews are also at the heart of most niche products and services. As long as people are looking for opinions, anything can be rated. Granted, reviews don't have to be on a rating scale as described in the activity. You can easily just segment them between good and bad, but people are easily swayed by popular opinion, so they have a significant impact.

Why we're using tag-based ratings and AddThis

The WordPress repository houses several ratings plugins that you can tweak, bend, and jimmy to suit your needs, if you're semi-decent at coding. Nevertheless, when it comes to WordPress and common sense, you should always try to find a simple solution, using features that are native to the CMS. Using a tag-based system to categorize your reviews makes it as easy to use on the backend as it does on the frontend. For example, you can access all your excellent reviews by accessing the URL `http://www.yourdomain.tld/tag/excellent/`. You can further style your tag-based reviews by creating tag template pages, which you can learn more about at `http://codex.wordpress.org/Tag_Templates`.

BuddyPress versus WP Symposium

If privacy is the Achilles' heel of BuddyPress, then this is where WP Symposium (WPS) shines. WPS is an alternative to BP in that it provides the same capabilities out of the box and then some. WPS also includes integrated forums, chat, galleries, events, and mobile access. BP, on the other hand, is also capable of the same extended features, but different developers produce all those plugins.

The issue with privacy

Privacy can make or break your site, literally. BP underwent several attempts at privacy solutions, but one popular plugin in particular, **BP Privacy Component**, would break occasionally with BP's release cycle. Again, the WordPress repository houses several plugins that can provide possible solutions, but none of them are core to BuddyPress. If you build a site that requires members' profiles to have privacy options and you rely on a plugin that is not core to BuddyPress, it leaves your site vulnerable to the possibility that you may lose that functionality, should the plugin developer decide to cease development. This can leave you with infuriated members, as you will undoubtedly try doing damage control and deal with sleep deprivation. WPS excels in this aspect, since it's built into core. The same developer who builds WPS also builds its multiple add-ons.

Single and multiple developers

WPS is just as easy to use and configure as BP. In some cases, it's even easier because you can easily move modules around, using shortcodes. WPS already ships with some features that are still being polished in the BP world, so there is quicker turnaround time when it comes to feature releases and the development roadmap. However, what makes this plugin so strong and nimble with its developer, Simon Goodchild, is also what makes it so weak. BuddyPress has a core of developers, an active support forum and at least two people on payroll at Automattic, the company that produces WordPress and BuddyPress. WPS is powered by donations and memberships, in comparison, which isn't ideal when it comes to building large sites, where there is access to a pool of developers all building on the same plugin.

What can I build with WPS?

WPS is a great alternative to BP, if you're building small niche community sites. The more registered site users you have, the more difficult it becomes to explain certain hiccups, should they encounter any technical issues. Once you branch out into the hundreds and thousands, in terms of member count, with a highly customized site, and you're relying on a plugin that has a single lead developer, there is a risk factor involved that you may not be able to resolve your issue in a timely manner. If you're dealing with several dozen people, it's typically a manageable issue. That said, you will still be able to complete the UGC activity. **Achievements** for BuddyPress currently relies on the BP plugin itself, so WPS users won't be able to take advantage of the gamification portion, using **Achievements**. Luckily, this plugin will eventually be able to run without BP, making it useable for WPS, as well.

Have a go hero

Countless sites already use a rewards program, so why shouldn't yours? What if you created a gift redemption page that's based on the point system used in **Achievement** for BuddyPress? What if you allowed users to include uploaded pictures using **Gravity Forms**? And what if you allowed random site visitors to rate and comment on those pictures? There are a myriad of possibilities that can engage users to have fun on your site. The key is to be creative in how you utilize the tools to drive those social connections. The connection has to make sense to your user; it does not revolve around a specific feature set.

Summary

This chapter introduced you to several inalienable truths to building social networking sites. These community sites are first and foremost about the community, their interaction, and site engagement, which you have control over.

In this chapter, we learned about the following:

- It only takes a few minutes to set up BuddyPress and WP Symposium, but it takes a lot of resources to build your community.
- There are ten excellent plugins that will speed up site development; nine of them are free.
- The concept of progressive profiling is an immense asset to producing more meaningful content.
- UGC also helps with SEO in that your site generates more content, which translates to more chances of search engines indexing your pages.
- Gamification can make your site more enjoyable to your users, which will attract even more users.
- The Facebook and AddThis API can lower the barrier of entry to your site.
- WPS is ideal for smaller niche communities.
- We also saw some interesting factoids on Mark Zuckerberg's Facemash and Facebook.

Now that we've learned about how to engage new members on your social networking site, we're going to give BuddyPress and WP Symposium another visit with community forums. Plus, we'll take a look at SimplePress, which is a forum plugin on steroids.

3
Community Forums for the Masses

If blogs were the precursors to WordPress, then forums were the precursors to bbPress, the popular forum software for WordPress. Both are producers of social media; the general public just hasn't seen them as such. It's easy to dismiss WordPress as just a blogging software, but in the last chapter, you learned you can easily download a few plugins and enable an immense Facebook-like social layer on top of your installation. Now, we'll take a look at forums, which provide another social layer where your visitors can connect with each other to exchange opinions on a variety of topics through bbPress and other forum alternatives.

Diving deeper into forums, or message boards, we'll take a look at exciting things such as:

- What you should expect when opening forums on your site
- How to create group forums using bbPress and BuddyPress
- Publishing WordPress posts to Twitter and automating the entire process
- Refining RSS Feed content using regex and RSS syndication
- Pros and cons of WP Symposium Forums and Simple:Press Forums
- Why automating as many processes as you can is important

Off we go...

Comments versus forums

Technologically and programmatically, forums aren't all too different from comments. Consider the following: a site visitor typically has to register with the site to post a message; the visitor responds to a particular topic in question; and, other people can reply to the visitor's response. It's an oversimplification of what really occurs on the backend what data gets stored where on your server but, at its crux, the processes involved are rather similar. Choosing which one to utilize as a main mode of communication can be tricky. Let's look into them a bit further.

When to use comments

WordPress sites typically have comments enabled by default, once they're initially set up. It's a good idea to keep this setting, as disabling comments will stifle visitor engagement. If you're using your WordPress site mainly as a blog, e-zine, or other publication site, you'll definitely want to use comments as your go-to form of communication, as each post or article will allow you to interact with your visitors. Also consider using the following plugins that will lower the barrier of entry for posting comments to your site:

- Disqus Comment System: This is a third-party comment platform, which will replace the WordPress commenting system. A minor drawback is that comments will not be stored on your server; however, as a benefit, visitors will be able to log in using their existing social networking site accounts such as Facebook, Twitter, and Yahoo. Learn more at http://disqus.com.

- Facebook AWD all in one: An all-inclusive plugin, Facebook AWD enables you to add a like button, activity feed, login button, like box, and comments all through Facebook. Just like the Disqus platform, none of the data is stored on your server, using these Facebook social plugins. Learn more at http://wordpress.org/extend/plugins/facebook-awd/.

- Social Login: If data ownership is a top priority for you, then this handy plugin by Claude Schlesser will allow your site visitors to log into your site using their Facebook, Google, Twitter, or WordPress credentials, while still letting you keep all of their comments and other data stored on your server.

When to use forums

Forums are great for managing evergreen content, or content with a long shelf life in one centralized part of your site. Site or blog posts tend to have a higher publishing frequency, often diluting the significance of older content within a matter of weeks, if not days. Most sites feature the most recent posts in the sidebar or they display them paginated on the homepage. If you publish about four to eight posts per week, there's a good chance that your visitors will not pay much attention to those posts and comments, as they'll get pushed back further with each passing day without the use of a plugin or marking selective forum posts as sticky.

When to use support forums

Forums do not need to focus on evergreen content. A common usage of forums also comes in the form of hosting content like *How can I properly limit main Activity Stream Loop to show five items per page?* as `BuddyPress.org` does with its support communities. Support forums are excellent tools that promote collaboration among site members when setting up a knowledge base. Site members can answer each other's questions and suggest new topics for discussion. In spite of this, forums do come with one big caveat—site moderation.

If you are setting up forums to provide support for a few applications, for example, be prepared to accommodate the amount of traffic you will receive. To put into perspective, BuddyPress support forums get flooded with new support questions every day, which requires a great deal of moderation. While some site members may be able to help each other, you will also need the resources to respond to unanswered questions that require more expert knowledge.

Watching out for common pitfalls

At their best, forums can supplement comments and further the discussion among active site members. At their worst, forums turn into incubators for trolls and flame wars, or newcomers who complain and initiate arguments. This will also require you to handle abrasive situations where new forum members may sound antagonizing. If you've followed the last chapter, you can ask someone from your BuddyPress network to help you with comment moderation.

Forums sound appealing and beneficial, but they can be completely unnecessary, especially if they're not maintained. If you are unsure whether to use them, ask yourself if you can use normal posts and comments instead. If you are still unsure, look at the activity on your site. Do your visitors comment often? Do your posts generate lots of comments? If the answer is no, you might have to work up to that level of engagement, before you roll out with your forums.

Another common pitfall when it comes to forums is inactivity. There is no worse forum than one that's ripe with out-dated posts or, worse, no activity at all. A dead forum is about as attractive to new site comers as a site that's covered with big and irrelevant ads. It's not socially engaging and can potentially hinder the entire site experience. This goes the same with blog posts that lack comments and even goes beyond WordPress, when talking about Facebook fan pages and Twitter accounts. If there is no recent activity in any account, regardless on what platform it occurs, the assumption is that you don't care all too much about interacting with your users.

In the upcoming activity, we'll look into how an active forum can actually help create content for your Twitter account, since content creation is a relative time-consuming practice.

Time for action – how to automatically display selective forum posts in Twitter

In the last two chapters, you learned how to automate e-mail campaigns and user-generated content submissions. In this in-depth activity, you'll learn how to spotlight forum content through Twitter, using forum posts as your content. You'll also automate this process using only selective sources and tweaking the content before it's **tweeted**, or posted to Twitter. For continuity, we'll assume that you're also running BuddyPress, as described in *Chapter 2*, *Building the Social Network: BuddyPress and WP Symposium*, and that you also own a Twitter account. You'll also learn how to clean up your automated posts in an optional Part 4 for this activity.

Part 1—setting up groups and forums for BuddyPress

Before we can post forum content to Twitter, bbPress needs to be configured. There are several steps to creating forums using bbPress and BuddyPress, since we're using the groups component for BP, but the good news is they are fairly straightforward:

1. In your dashboard, navigate to **Component** under **BuddyPress** and click on the **Forums** tab near the top.

2. To allow for the greatest amount of control, click on the **Install Group Forums** button, as this will keep your members' conversations separated into distinct areas.

3. Next, you'll be prompted for a new bbPress installation, so continue by clicking on the **Complete Installation** button. Depending on your server permissions, you may receive another prompt to create a bb-config.php file, which you can easily create using Notepad (or TextEdit for OSX) and upload using FileZilla. You should now be able to visit your **Forums** page at http://www.yourdomain.tld/forums/.

4. To create your first forum, you'll need to create a group first, as you selected the group forums option in Step 2. Navigate to `http://www.yourdomain.tld/groups/` and click on the **Create a Group** button next to the **Groups Directory** heading.

5. Fill out the **Group Name** and **Group Description**, and continue with the group creation by using the default options for **Privacy Options** and **Group Invitation**. **This is a public group** and **All group members**, respectively. To speed up the process, you can click on the **Next Step** button for Step 3 and the **Finish** button for Step 4. You can always go back and make edits to your groups later.

6. Next, visit your **Forums** page at `http://www.yourdomain.tld/forums/` and click on the **New Topic** button next to the **Forums Directory** heading.

7. Fill out all the fields. The **Title** will become the heading for the forum; the **Content** will become the first thread of the forum; and, the **Tags** will become the meta data for the forum. Also, be sure to select the group you created in Step 6 from the group drop-down selection before clicking on the **Post Topic** button.

8. Visit your newly created forum and post some replies to get a feel of how it functions:

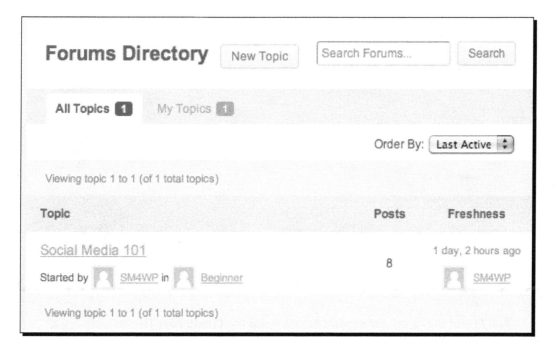

Part 2—creating tweets through forum content

In this part, you'll learn how to publish content from your WordPress site and post it through your Twitter account. To do this, you will need to register for a free Twitter account, if you don't already have one, and then create a Twitter application that connects to your WP site. This part requires that you follow all the steps in this particular order to reduce your workload:

1. First, we're going to add the functionality to post to Twitter from your WordPress site by navigating to **Add New** under **Plugins** and searching for a **WP to Twitter**. Install and activate the plugin.

2. Navigate to **WP to Twitter** under **Settings** and follow the steps to connect Twitter to your WordPress site by first logging on to Twitter's application registration page at `https://dev.twitter.com/apps/new`. Give your application an appropriate name and description, and use the URL for your site in the **WebSite** field, as shown in the following screenshot. The **Callback URL** is not required, so we'll skip that for now, as you can always edit it later:

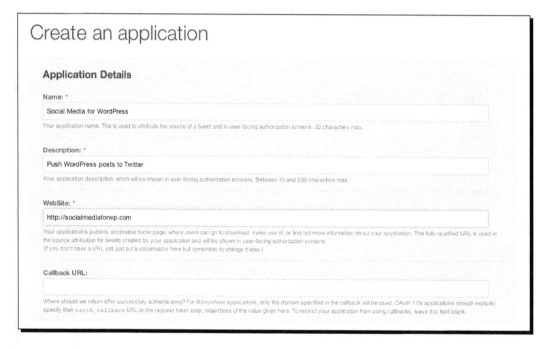

3. Accept the terms and conditions, and press the **Create your Twitter application** button.

4. Once your Twitter application has been created, navigate to the **Settings** tab near the top and select **Read and Write** for the **Access level** under **Application Type**. This will allow WordPress to post information to Twitter. Be sure to press the **Update this Twitter application's settings** button near the bottom of the page to save your changes.

5. Next, press the **Details** tab near the top and press the **Create my access token** button in the **Your access token** section near the bottom. This will create the **Access Token** as well as the **Access Token Secret**. Make sure the **Access level** shows **Read and Write**, as shown in the screenshot. If it does not, repeat Step 4 and make sure **Read and Write** is selected and create a new token with the updated settings:

6. Back in WordPress, fill in all the appropriate information to connect Twitter with your site and press the **Connect to Twitter** button in **WP to Twitter** under **Settings**.

7. Once connected, make sure to uncheck **Update when a post is edited** under **Basic Settings**, as you don't want to tweet old content. Keep all other default values. Also, select **Use WordPress as a URL shortener** from the **Choose your short URL service** drop-down selection, as you don't want to display long URLs in your tweets; use bitly if you have an account instead, as you'll be able to easily track views this way. Press the **Save WP | Twitter options** button to save your changes.

8. Navigate to **Categories** under **Posts** and create a new category named **relay**.

9. Last, navigate back to **WP to Twitter** under **Settings** and select relay from the **Limit Updating Categories** section near the bottom, so that only content stored in that category will be tweeted. Press the **Set Categories** button to save your changes.

10. You can test this tweeting functionality by creating a new post and selecting the **relay** category before you publish it. We're not pulling content from your forum and the tweeting process isn't automated yet, so we'll cover that in Part 3.

Twitter tips

You can use hashtags (for example, #socialmedia), retweets (for example, RT), and even at-naming (@socialmedia4wp) in your text for new post updates: field, which will automatically create the links once your post is published on WordPress and sent to Twitter. For more information about hashtags and Twitter basics, check out these links:

Twitter 101: How should I get started using Twitter?: `http://support.twitter.com/groups/31-twitter-basics/topics/104-welcome-to-twitter-support/articles/215585-twitter-101-how-should-i-get-started-using-twitter`

What Are hashtags ("#" Symbols)?: `http://support.twitter.com/articles/49309-what-are-hashtags-symbols`

The Twitter glossary: `http://support.twitter.com/articles/166337-the-twitter-glossary`

Part 3—automating and customizing tweets with WordPress

In this last part, you'll use Yahoo! Pipes again just as you did in *Chapter 1, Share it the Easy Way*. This time, you'll use the free service to customize the output for your automated tweets. Let's get started:

1. BuddyPress doesn't come with very many RSS feeds by default, so we'll add a few more by going to **Add New** under **Plugins** and searching for **BP Lotsa Feeds**. Install and activate the plugin. The plugin doesn't come with any backend options. Instead, it allows you to access your site's added RSS feeds based on this structure:

Feed Content	Feed URL
Individual Members	
Network-wide comments by an individual member	`http://www.yourdomain.tld/members/username/activity/comments/feed`
Network-wide blog posts by an individual member	`http://www.yourdomain.tld/members/username/activity/blogposts/feed`
Activity updates by an individual member	`http://www.yourdomain.tld/members/username/activity/updates/feed`
An individual member's friendship connections	`http://www.yourdomain.tld/members/username/activity/friendships/feed`
Forum topics started by an individual member	`http://www.yourdomain.tld/members/username/activity/forumtopics/feed`
Forum replies by an individual member	`http://www.yourdomain.tld/members/username/activity/forumreplies/feed`
All forum activity by a member	`http://www.yourdomain.tld/members/username/activity/forums/feed`
Individual Groups	
A group's activity updates	`http://www.yourdomain.tld/groups/groupname/updates/feed`
New forum topics in a given group	`http://www.yourdomain.tld/groups/groupname/forumtopics/feed`
Forum replies in a given group	`http://www.yourdomain.tld/groups/groupname/forumreplies/feed`

Feed Content	Feed URL
All forum activity in a given group	`http://www.yourdomain.tld/ groups/groupname/forums/feed`
A group's new members	`http://www.yourdomain.tld/ groups/groupname/membership/feed`
Forums	
Individual forum topic posts	`http://www.yourdomain.tld/ groups/groupname/forum/topic/ topicslug/feed`

2. To view network-wide comments by a member named John, for example, you would visit `http://www.yourdomain.tld/members/john/activity/comments/ feed`

3. Next, we'll add another plugin by navigating to **Add New** under **Plugins** and searching for a plugin labelled **FeedWordPress**. Install and activate the plugin. If you encounter any activation issues, deactivate all plugins first and then activate **FeedWordPress**. Then, re-activate all your other plugins that you're using.
   At this point, you could use any of the feeds from Step 1 and feed them into **FeedWordPress**, so that they would be posted to Twitter. But we'll go a step further by tweaking the tweet content a bit.

4. In a new browser window, log on to `http://pipes.yahoo.com/pipes/`. If you've followed along since *Chapter 1*, use your login credentials to create a new pipe. If you've skipped to this chapter, create a free Yahoo! account or use your Google or Facebook credentials to log in. Then, click on the **Create a pipe** button.

5. Drag the **Fetch Feed** module on the left window pane under the **Sources** header to **workspace**, which is the big, light-blue space located to the right. In the empty field, enter the location of the feed for the forum that you created in Step 6 of Part 1, (for example,. `http://www.yourdomain.tld/groups/beginner/forum/topic/ bbpress/feed`).

6. Since the feed's description item is the essence of the content for your tweet, we'll remap this data to the feed's title, since this is what **FeedWordPress** uses to create your tweet. Simply drag the **Create RSS** module on the left window pane to the workspace and match all of the drop-down items to their corresponding fields (that is, **item.description** for **Description**, **item.link** for **Link**, and so on). Change only the **Title** field, which gets the drop-down selection of **item.description** you'll use **item. description** twice for the **Title** and the **Description** fields. This way, the **Description** becomes the **Title**.

7. Now, drag the **Regex** (regular expression) module to the workspace area to clean up the **Title** content, which currently has a bunch of HTML and other gibberish, as it was pulled directly from the RSS feed's description item (the content of the blog post).

8. To get rid of the HTML tags, click on the **Rule** link and select **item.title** from the drop-down selection and enter < . * ? > for the **replace** field, as shown in the following screenshot. Leave the **with** field empty, so that all HTML tags will get deleted. Be sure to select the **g** option (radio button) to the right to have this rule applied globally for all instances of the **item.title** content:

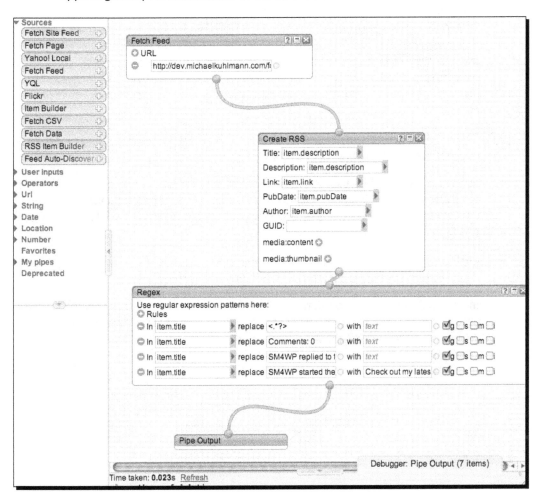

9. Create a few new rules to delete and replace the **item.title** content with more conversational language. For example, repeat Step 7 and enter `Comments: 0` in the **replace** field to delete all instances of `Comments: 0` in your tweet, since that is irrelevant. You can also replace all instances of username who started the forum topic in the group name, where the user name, forum topic, and group name correspond to your respective names. Simply enter **Check out my latest post at** in the **with** field when you do this, so you essentially replace one set of words with a new set of words. Using the previous example, the tweet will result in **Check out my latest post at http://www.yourdomain.tld/?p=734**.

10. In order to create and run this pipe, you will have to connect, or draw, the pipe from one module to the other. First, connect the **Fetch Feed** module to the **Create RSS** module. Then, connect the **Create RSS** module to the **Regex** module. Finally, connect the **Regex** module to the **Pipe Output** module. To run your pipe, click on the **Pipe Output** title bar, which will highlight it. In the **Debugger** window located at the very bottom, you will see a **Refresh** link that will display your custom content once clicked.

11. Click on the **Save** button located toward the top-left of your window and give it an appropriate name, such as **Group Tweets**.

12. To get the URL for this custom RSS feed, which you will use as material for **FeedWordPress**, click on the **Back To My Pipes** near the top to list your Yahoo! Pipe. Click on the **Publish** link by hovering over your pipe to produce a publicly accessible RSS feed for this data.

13. Click on the orange RSS icon labelled **Get as RSS** to get the link to this feed and copy it somewhere, as you will need it for your **FeedWordPress**.

14. In your WordPress dashboard, navigate to **Syndication** and enter the RSS feed address from Step 12 into the **New Source** field within the **Syndicated Sources** section. Be sure to press the **Add** button and press the **Use this feed** button on the subsequent page.

By using Twitter's API, you may exceed your Twitter limit. This means, when you try to access your Twitter account and your forum has lots of activity, you will not be able to use your Twitter account through Twitter's own website. If you don't want to run into the issue of not being able to tweet through Twitter's website, create a new Twitter account that corresponds to your site's forums.

Remember, the more communication channels or, in this case, Twitter accounts that you can open up for your visitors, the higher the likelihood there will be for visitors to reach out to you. For example, CNN's and reporters of `AllThingsD.com` each have their own Twitter account instead of a global news account. Some companies append a topic name to their main Twitter names including Twitter itself (that is, @twitterbusiness), which allows followers to inform them that they're still related to the main name (that is, @twitter). Alternatively, you can tweet through WordPress permanently.

(Optional) Part 4—automatically deleting duplicate Twitter content

Since you're re-publishing forum content for each tweet that's created, you'll have some duplicate content on your WordPress site. You'll also notice that your regular posts will be shuffled with the tweet posts. This may or may not be an issue for you. If it is, follow this activity, which will teach you how to automatically clean up your posts.

1. In your **WordPress** dashboard, navigate to **Add New** under **Plugins** and search for **Auto prune posts**. Install and activate the plugin.

2. Modify the settings for this plugin by navigating to **Auto prune posts** under **Plugins**, which will display an array of options.

3. Select the **relay** category that you created in Step 8 of Part 2 from the drop-down selection, and enter 1 for the **time** drop-down selection, which should be in **hours**. This will delete the relayed posts from Part 3 after one hour. Be sure to press the **Add** settings button to save your changes.

What just happened?

You just created a process in which selective forum posts are published to Twitter. First, you enabled bbPress, the forum plugin for WordPress, to set up forums based on groups. Then, you created a simple Twitter application, which tied your site to Twitter to publish tweets based on your WordPress posts. To automate this process, you also created a Yahoo! Pipe, which took your forum content and tweaked it a bit to sound more fitting for Twitter. Last, you learned how to automatically clean up some of your WordPress content.

Keep your tweets conversational

The main reason we used Yahoo! Pipes was two-fold. First, we were able to leverage this service so we could segment the content. Secondly, we were able to change the tone of the syndicated content. Truth be told, you can skip Part 2 and just use the direct RSS feed produced by bbPress for **FeedWordPress**. However, the resulting tweet would have been something like **Admin replied to the forum topic Social Media for WordPress in the group Beginner** for every forum reply. This is hardly ideal, as Twitter is a conversational media. It's a stream of conscience, a tweet. The tweet needs to sound organic, not like an automaton that posts forum statuses. Together with the granularity in feeds provided by BP Lotsa Feeds and Yahoo! Pipes' multiple modules, you have a lot of creative reign to allow your voice to reverberate on Twitter. Here are some helpful pointers to sound more like a seasoned Twitterer:

- **Stick to lower-case tweets**: Tweets are meant to be brief bursts of information. Using upper-case sounds like you're screaming. Using title-case looks like you spent half an hour figuring out the best way to present 140 characters to your followers. There are always exceptions, but the majority of tweets will be lower-case.

- **Use hashtags whenever and wherever appropriate**: Think of hashtags as inbound linking for Twitter. If you can think of popular hashtags that fit with your tweets, be sure to use them.

- **Acknowledge your followers**: If you have followers, who mention you in a tweet, reciprocate that action. If you have followers, who mention you in a tweet on a Friday, take it a step further and acknowledge them using the `#followfriday` or `#ff hashtag`.

Benefits of automating processes

In the first chapter, you learned about e-mail marketing automation and, in the second chapter, you learned about automating user-generated content submissions. In this chapter, you learned about automating content syndication. The reason you are learning how to improve these processes by automating them is time management.

It takes a lot of time and planning to come up with a brilliant strategy that will lure in new visitors and get them to engage with each other on your site. More importantly, it takes equal amounts of time to do it on a regular basis to grow your site. Tweeting original content is always more effective than syndicating something that may not resonate with the majority of your followers. On the other hand, tweeting syndicating content is more effective than not tweeting at all.

You will have to find the balance for the ratio of irrelevant content that gets automatically tweeted. If the RSS feed you've created in Yahoo! Pipes is too broad for your Twitter followers, you may find yourself losing a few followers in the process. Don't worry and keep polishing your pipe. Tweeting content that is 100 percent relevant to 100 percent of your followers, 100 percent of the time, is a futile approach. Instead, try to get some traction by listening to what your visitors deem as hot forum topics on your site, so you hone your tweets in on a more fruitful discussion when you syndicate that content on Twitter. Besides, Twitter boasts upwards of 100 million active users, so there are plenty of people who will find you interesting.

Pop quiz – forum fun

1. bbPress requires running BuddyPress on your site.

    a. True

    b. False

2. Group forums do not have any privacy settings.

    a. True

    b. False

3. FeedWordPress is a content syndication plugin.

    a. True

    b. False

4. Regex stands for regular expression and is capable of matching text.

    a. True

    b. False

5. It's never a good idea to segment content.

    a. True

    b. False

Have a go hero

You've learned about all the steps involved to automatically post your website content to the most popular micro blogging service in the world. But you've also done more than that. You've learned about content syndication and regular expressions. What if you syndicated the user-generated content that you've learned in *Chapter 2*. What if you used **Regex** to fine-tune the RSS feed you piped together in *Chapter 1*, when you created your automated e-mail campaign? What is you used Achievements for BuddyPress to reward people with relevant content that you could tweet on their behalf? With each new activity you learn, there is a multiplying factor that allows you to switch and combine processes from all chapters up to this point. How can you push what you've just learned to create something new?

WP Symposium Forums and Simple:Press

In the previous chapter, you learned about a BuddyPress alternative called WP Symposium. This relatively new WordPress extension ships with a native forum module, so the setup time is quick and easy. Simple:Press, in comparison, has been around for several years and is maintained by a group of people. It's also feature-rich, which makes it a great contender for bbPress. Both WPS Forums and Simple:Press forums produce RSS feeds, which you can use to complete the activities outlined in this chapter. For more information about the respective plugins, read on.

WP Symposium forums

Out of the box, WPS Forums comes with a customizable voting mechanism that allows users to vote on forum posts. This functionality would take yet another plugin to re-create in BuddyPress. Additionally, another gamification feature known as **Forum Ranks** allows you to assign titles like *Emperor* or *Peasant* to your users, based on a point system that keeps track of how many posts they create. Users also have the option of sharing posts through LinkedIn, Bebo, and MySpace to name a few other social networking sites. Again, re-creating this functionality in BP would require another plugin or custom function.

WPS Forums, design-wise, are very sparse and similar to BuddyPress, which make them easy to style, if you have a good grasp of CSS. Some of the WPS features also utilize modal windows, or lightboxes, which you may or may not prefer over more traditional viewing. A major drawback, which can be attributed to the early developmental stage of this plugin, is the lack of granular RSS feeds like you've used for BuddyPress. Because of this, you would most likely need to create a few more regex rules and RSS filters for automating tweets that pull content from your forums. More information on WPS can be found at `http://www.wpswiki.com`.

Simple:Press

Since **Simple:Press Forums (SPF)** has been around for a few years, all the major kinks have been ironed out. SPF are entirely feature-rich, ranging from user profiles and groups to component settings that get as specific as private messaging statistics. Just like WPS, Simple:Press has its own dedicated wiki online at `http://wiki.simple-press.com`. Unlike WPS, Simple:Press has acquired a group of developers, who frequent the support forums to assist with bugs and feature requests. Perhaps, the best feature is that Simple:Press profiles work with BuddyPress extended profiles. So while you may not want to use bbPress for your BuddyPress installation, you can still use BP along with SPF.

Aesthetically, SPF are more in line with what your typical forums look like post time stamp, online status indication, post forum topic tags, and the like are all thrown together. You can even download forum skins to further match the branding of your site. However, trying to create your own forum skin can be a bit laborious, because of the intricacy of this forum platform. In fact, it is because of this innate complexity that SPF does take a considerable amount of time to properly set up. Unlike, bbPress and WPS Forums, SPF may be a bit too much and overwhelming for you, if all you want is a simple plugin that's easy to use on the frontend as it is on the backend. Still, it is a viable alternative worth considering, if you're planning on using more advanced features like sub-forums.

Summary

This chapter continues with activities that automate time-consuming processes. You've also learned a few more tricks, using Yahoo! Pipes to shape RSS feeds. Above all, you learned how to build relationships with forums and, therefore, made it more socially engaging.

To refresh on the main points, we've covered the following:

You can use posts and comments instead of a dedicated forum

- Forums require a great deal of resources and moderation
- bbPress can be used as a stand-alone forum or it can be paired with BuddyPress
- You can push WordPress content to Twitter automatically
- You can enable multiple RSS feeds for your site
- Regex is extremely powerful in moulding your content
- FeedWordPress is versatile in that you can use it as a relay plugin

Up until this point, you have only grazed on the topic of memberships through the concept of gamification and integrating forums. There is much more to explore when adding a membership section to your site, so we'll save that for the next chapter.

4
VIP Memberships

What do John Lennon, Jim Henson, and Les Paul have in common? They were all featured on Google's homepage as doodles, which is the search company's homage for their tremendous contribution to society. Several times a year, Google selects very important people to recognize and validate through these doodles. In fact, these drawings have become so popular that a library of them is now available online (`http://www.google.com/doodles/`*).*

Validation is also front and centre of why there are so many exclusive clubs and memberships. We have an innate desire to be validated and we satiate that appetite by unlocking badges, for example, on foursquare, a location-based social networking site. We may also invite friends, colleagues or acquaintances on Google+ to make them feel more entitled. Sometimes, we even have to register with a site, as is the case with Facebook, to access the walled garden of social connections. In any case, social media sites tend to gravitate toward some form of membership.

Before we delve into the activities in building interactive memberships, here's what we'll learn:

- Why customer value proposition, sustainability, and timing matter
- How to set up memberships and make category-specific content restrictions applicable only to non-members
- Key opportunities to mention your other social networking accounts on our site
- How to implement page-specific custom scripts like a countdown timer
- More ways to reward site members for using our site

Let's bring some of these ideas to fruition.

Three important facets of membership sites

Although you can dissect a successful membership-based site into pieces, there are three vital elements. What do I get out of registering for this site? Why should I register now? How will this site impact me two weeks from now? These are all simple and fair enough questions. Let's get down to the nitty-gritty.

Customer value proposition

Creating membership-based sites is tricky, because there is a natural expectation that a visitor or customer will receive something of value by registering for a site. If there is a low incentive for registering for your site, don't expect too many signups. The opposite is true, as well. A site that offers a full album in exchange for site registration will fare better than a site that only offers one song from the same album. **Customer Value Proposition (CVP)** is not rocket science, but it's a concept that you need to grasp to grow your site. What you perceive as great value might not necessarily be in line with what your prospective members expect. CVP also doesn't dictate that you need to put a price tag on the value that you're proposing; it merely suggests that what you are proposing will be useful and relevant to your site visitors. If you are unsure whether you are proposing something valuable on your site, in exchange for the time and effort it takes to complete a site registration, ask a neighbour, co-worker, or other acquaintance some of these questions:

- What aspect of this site would make you register for it? If you wouldn't register for it, why not?
- Would you recommend this site to your friends or family?
- How can the membership be more compelling?
- Would you ever consider paying a fee to keep your membership?

Regardless of what people say, you have to be open to constructive criticism. Throwing all feedback by the wayside typically means that you are not prepared to embark on what you are doing. Last, be honest with yourself and try not to ask your parents, best friend, or spouse for this type of critical feedback, unless you're certain they won't be shy in trying to poke holes at your ideas. The more uncensored, truthful opinions you can collect, the more your site and membership will be polished.

Timing

Roman philosopher Lucius Annaeus Seneca is often quoted as saying, *Luck is what happens when preparation meets opportunity*. While you don't have to be lucky to offer memberships, you do have to be strategic in how you open up site registrations. For example, you wouldn't suddenly offer a VIP membership in the form of a paywall, if there weren't any significant differences in your own freely available content or that of a competitor. You would, however, open limited VIP membership registrations on December 12, 2012 that offered premium content such as videos, downloads, and other goodies. In this example, the advantages are two-fold:

◆ First, you would spark a sense of urgency and exclusivity by using the terms *limited registrations*.

◆ Second, the registration date would allow you to market the VIP membership during the holiday season, when people are already on a spending spree. Plus, you would be able to make it easier for prospective VIP members to memorize this registration date by advertising it as a *12.12.12* event.

Again, it's not rocket science per se, but you do have to take the opportunity and be prepared with a plan of action. You only get one first impression when you pitch your membership to your visitors, so try to schedule the registration period during a time when there is a significant change on your site—a site launch, re-design, newly added section, partnership, or any other big announcement. This way, it appears more like a bonus feature than a gateway to profile your users. If you plan on keeping membership registrations open indefinitely, be sure to keep the content fresh on the page that outlines the benefits of registering for your site. Some sites update rotating testimonials whereas others may feature recently registered users to prevent the membership opportunity from looking stale.

Holidays and other celebratory days are extremely helpful when it comes to timing, as they allow you to spotlight your membership section. If you charge for a premium membership, for example, you can always promote discounted specials through Facebook, Twitter, or any other social media networking site. Pairing Earth Day with news that your sites are running on energy efficient servers, for instance, would allow you to advertise something like *Our community is all about green energy*. You could even build a whole green campaign around membership signups, utilizing videos (http://www.youtube.com) and photo galleries (http://www.flickr.com) to paint a more telling story.

Sustainability

We've figured out a way to entice your prospective customers to register with our site, but what now? When it comes to site memberships, sustainability is a blanket term that incorporates long-term growth coupled with **loyalty marketing**—the practice in which you retain your customers, or site members, by focusing and delivering customer satisfaction, which, in turn, leads to an increased ROI.

CVP and timing can only take you so far. In the previous chapter, we allowed our users to be proactive in shaping the content of our site through their own submissions. In *Chapter 2*, *Building the Social Network: BuddyPress and WP Symposium*, we learned how to leverage BuddyPress to engage our members by introducing achievements that can be unlocked to gain badges, or rewards points. When we first started this book, we also discovered building engagement is near impossible, unless there is relevant content that applies to our audience.

We come full-circle, now that we're honing in on building site memberships. Sustainability, at this juncture, means repetition. It means that we cannot rely on a one-off piece of content, an interesting blog post, a great album, or an amazing product to engage our members. It means that we cannot procrastinate on our content, if we want people to actively talk about it. The web works at warp speed, so it's imperative that we churn out good content on a regular basis. It can be absolutely time-consuming. But that's also why we've learned how to automate a lot processes to dedicate more resources to content in previous chapters. Good content will always remain at the forefront of sustaining your user retention.

Time for action – how to open limited membership registrations and reward users

For this activity, we will start off by using WordPress' official **Twenty Eleven** theme and four plugins—**HeadSpace2 SEO**, **WP Show IDs**, **S2 Member,** and **Cube Points**:

Part 1—setting up member-accessible content

In this part, we will configure the S2 Member plugin to block content for site visitors that have not registered with the site yet:

1. In your dashboard, navigate to **Add New** under **Plugins** and search for **S2 Member**. Install and activate the plugin.

2. Next, add a new plugin called **WP Show IDs** by repeating the directions in Step 1. This plugin simply displays the ID associated with each post, page, and category.

3. Now we'll create the login welcome page, which is the page a member will see upon logging in, by navigating to **Add New** under **Pages**. Title it **Login Welcome Page**. Since this is the first page that members will see each time, take the opportunity to let them connect with you on Facebook, Twitter, LinkedIn, or any of your other social media networking accounts, by mentioning this in your **content** field. See the following screenshot for an example:

4. Create a new page but, this time, give it a title of **Membership Options Page**. This will be the page non-members, or the general public, will be redirected to when they attempt to access any content that's restricted to members. It can also double as a payment gateway page, if you choose to sell subscriptions to access content. Again, be sure to highlight your other social media network accounts by mentioning this in your content field like in the previous step.

5. Navigate to **Categories** under **Posts** and create a new category called **VIP**. We'll use this to restrict access to posts filed under this category. Be sure to jot down the ID of this category when you create it, as you'll need it later. The ID is located in the last column to the right of the category list.

6. Configure S2 Member to recognize the VIP category as a restricted category, only accessible to registered members, by navigating to **Restriction Options** under **S2 Member**. Click the **Category Access Restrictions** section and type in 3, the ID you obtained by the previous step, under the **Categories That Require Level #0 Or Higher:** field. Be sure to press the **Save All Changes** button at the bottom to save your changes.

7. Since S2 Member isn't set up yet to use the two pages that you've created in Steps 3 and 4, we'll now configure this by navigating to **General Options** under **S2 Member**. Under the **Login Welcome Page** section, select the page that you created in Step 3 from the drop-down selection. Under the **Members Options Page**, select the page that you had created in Step 4 from the drop-down selection. Be sure to press the **Save All Changes** button to save your changes.

8. As an optional step, you can test your VIP membership by creating a new post and categorizing it under **VIP**. View the page to simulate the logged in state. Then, log out and try to access that post again. If you're redirected to your **Members Options Page**, it's properly configured.

> Everything still remains customizable, so if you change your page titles, post contents, category labels, or slugs, just be sure to update your settings accordingly under the **General Options** and **Restriction Options** sections in S2 Member.

Part 2—adding a countdown to your members options page

We'll use the **Members Options Page** that you created in the previous part and dress it up a bit with a timer that counts down to a set time. The countdown script itself will be readily available, but we'll use the **HeadSpace2 SEO** plugin to implement it:

1. Download the countdown JavaScript and accompanying CSS file at
   `http://socialmediaforwp.com/downloads/countdown-script/`.

2. To host the files from the previous step on your WordPress site, navigate to **Add New** under **Media** and press the **Select Files** button to upload them. After they've been uploaded, press the **Show** link on both files and write down the file URL, as you'll need them later.

3. Navigate to **Add New** under **Plugins** and search for **HeadSpace2 SEO**. Install and activate the plugin.

4. Edit the **Members Options Page** that you had created in Part 1, by navigating to **All Pages** under **Pages** and clicking on the **Edit** link, after you hover over the page name.

5. Under the **content** field on your page, you will notice a new section labeled **HeadSpace**. Click on the **advanced** link on the bottom-right corner to reveal the **JavaScript** and **Stylesheets** fields. Enter the file links from Step 2 for the respective fields. The `.js` file path should be entered in the **JavaScript** field, and the `.css` file path should be entered in the **Stylesheets** field.

6. Finally, paste the following code snippet into the **content** field wherever you want to display the countdown timer. In the following screenshot, this snippet is located above the first line of text:

```
<div id="countdowncontainer">
<script type="text/javascript">
var futuredate=new cdtime("countdowncontainer", "December 12, 2012
12:12:12")
```

```
futuredate.displaycountdown("days", formatresults)
</script>
</div>
```

7. The highlighted part indicates the time this script will count down to the exact second. This is a relative date, which means it is relative to the time the computer is set to. In the preceding example, the timer counts down to December 12, 2012 at 12:12PM and 12 seconds for any time zone. To adjust the target date, change the values for the month, day, year, and time, using the 24-hour time format.

8. This script will not stop registrations for you, once the target date has reached; it will just display a message, stating that registrations are closed. You will have to manually close registrations within the **Settings** section, in order to accomplish this task. Using the CSS styles you've uploaded in Step 2, your countdown container should be orange with white text, counting down to a set time that you've configured in Step 6:

Become a VIP Member

401 days 2 hours 21 minutes 50 seconds left to sign up for this site!

You're trying to access content that only the cool folks can see. Bummer. Luckily, it's easy for you to become part of the VIP simply by **registering at our site**.

WANNA KNOW WHAT WE'RE UP?

Subscribe to us on Facebook, follow us on Twitter, connect with us on LinkedIn or watch some of our YouTube videos. Just click on any of the buttons below.

Modifying the target date countdown message

By default, the message that appears after the countdown script has finished counting down to the target date is as follows: *Registration is closed. Visit us regularly for updates!* You can easily edit this message by opening up the `countdown.js` file in a text editor, searching for that string of words and replacing the text. Consider the opportunity to allow site members to follow you on Twitter, as well. For example, you may want to display *Registration is closed. Follow us at @YourTwitterName on Twitter*. Whatever you decide, be sure to reference the most recent version in the HeadSpace file URL field to reflect your edits, if you're using copies of the JavaScript file.

Part 3—rewarding your site members

In this part, you'll reward your site members for registering with your site and you'll also reward them for each time they log in:

1. As there is no core functionality within WordPress or S2 Member to reward points to register and log in for your site, we'll add it by installing a new plugin. Navigate to **Add New** under **Plugins** and search for **CubePoints**. Install and activate the plugin.

2. To enable rewards points for registrations and logins, navigate to **Modules** under **CubePoints** and click on the **Activate** link for the **Daily Points** module.

3. Click on the **Activate** link for the **Notify** module to enable visual notifications whenever your users earn points.

4. If you do not want to associate a dollar value for each point earned, as it is set by default, navigate to **Configure** under **CubePoints** and delete the $ (dollar) symbol from the **Prefix for display of points:** field. Be sure to press the **Update Options** button toward the bottom to save your changes. You can also temporarily change the value to 1 for the **Time interval for awarding points** field under **Daily Points** to test out the two modules that you activated, but be sure to revert your changes before going live.

5. To display the users' CubePoints, navigate to **Widgets** under **Appearance** and drag the CubePoints widget into the main sidebar. If you access your site as a visitor, you should see a section labeled **My Points** with your current point count. You should also see a notification in the upper-right corner of your screen, as shown in the following screenshot:

Be sure to tell your site visitors and users about your reward system, as they will not know how the points and notifications work. The best place to mention this is on the **Members Options Page**, where you outline the benefits of registering for your site. Additionally, you can dedicate a whole page to your rewards system, which further details that aspect of your site and link it from the **Members Options Page**.

What just happened?

In Part 1, we learned how to make certain content inaccessible to non-registered members. We also took the opportunity to cross-promote our social networking accounts on the **Members Options Page** as well as the **Login Welcome** page. In the next part, we learned how to emphasize the registration process by including a countdown script. In Part 3, we rewarded our users for registering and logging into our site.

S2 Member and CubePoints

S2 Member in conjuction with CubePoints provided us with an alternative solution to BuddyPress and Achievements. There is no one right answer when it comes to finding the perfect set of membership functionality to complement our site. For some, the BuddyPress and Achievements combination may be too much maintenance, even if it is scaled down to a few activated components. For others, S2 Member with CubePoints might seem too limiting to start out a new site launch. However, the main advantage with S2 Member and CubePoints is that they both integrate with BuddyPress. We can start out with just a basic WordPress installation, go through the activities in this chapter and, months down the road, revisit *Chapter 2, Building the Social Network: BuddyPress and WP Symposium*, and implement some of those ideas to extend our site even further.

Both the S2 Member and CubePoints plugins feature a comprehensive list of features. The activities in this chapter merely scratched the surface in what you can do. For a better look at the scope of available functionality, consider this:

Downloading the example code for this book

You can download the example code files for all Packt books you have purchased from your account at http://www.PacktPub.com. If you purchased this book elsewhere, you can visit http://www.PacktPub.com/support and register to have the files e-mailed directly to you.

S2 Member	CubePoints
Free subscribers and four primary membership levels	Multiple ways to earn points through registering, commenting, logging in daily, writing posts and more
PayPal integration for membership levels	Display points with widgets
Customizable membership labels	
Support for an unlimited number of Custom Capability packages, which allow you to create an unlimited number of membership packages, all with different capabilities and prices	User-to-user donations to cultivate more engagement with each other
	Log all your point transactions
Protection capability for pages, posts, tags, categories, URIs, URI word fragments, and URI replacement codes for BuddyPress	User ranks which can automatically assigned based on the amount of points users have
	Easy user management
Specific post/page, Buy Now access, and portions of content within posts/pages/themes/plugins	Tracking for user points, which users to access point balance, and recent transactions
	Integration with other plugins

More detailed information on S2 Member and CubePoints can be found at
`http://s2member.com/` and `http://cubepoints.com/`

Another foray into gamification

Chapter 2, introduced us to Achievements for BuddyPress that made user engagement more entertaining by turning it into a game of earning points and badges. CubePoints features more functionality, in this regard, and combining it with S2 Member takes this idea up a notch. There are a myriad of possible combinations to attract our users to connect with each other such as the following:

- Visitors on our site can pay for a certain membership level and attain a badge
- We can create a membership level where we can hand pick several special members to promote our site for us through other social networking sites and be rewarded in the process
- An elite group of our members can represent us and our brand on our behalf for a full day, pending on our users' rank or points

The possibilities are virtually infinite and, starting out, you will most likely have to limit yourself in becoming overzealous to what you'll want to offer to your site members. Just remember *validation is key*. Make them feel as special as Google does with its doodles. There are a ton of sites requiring users to register, but only a handful of them take the time and initiative to engage and reward their members to establish a meaningful and loyal following.

Pop quiz – in the VIP

1. All memberships have to be VIP Memberships.

    a. True

    b. False

2. CubePoints is an excellent alternative to BuddyPress.

    a. True

    b. False

3. S2 Member supports paid memberships.

    a. True

    b. False

4. CVP is an acronym for constant value perimeter.

    a. True

    b. False

5. BuddyPress integrates with CubePoints and S2 Member.

    a. True

    b. False

Have a go hero

It is possible to use UGC, combine it with a MailChimp campaign and reward your VIP members by interacting with the campaign. Everything is doable, but you have to strategize first, and you always have to use your own voice. For example, if your niche site deals with renegades and mavericks (that is, bungee jumpers, drift car racers, or parkour practitioners), you could easily reward users for doing something wrong or risky. CubePoints and Achievements merely provide a set of functionality for you to distribute points and badges based on an action. That action is always predefined by you and needs to appeal to your users. Think of it this way, what is something your site user can do that validates him or her as someone who is part of your community? If you can find the answer to that, be sure to have those rewards ready.

Summary

Pop-ups, rewards points, and badges don't make up a site, and they certainly don't make it social. What matters is how site members connect with you and vice versa. Social media only comes into play when your members have something to share, when there is something worthwhile sharing. Sometimes that something is worthwhile blocking through memberships for exclusivity.

Rewinding back to the beginning of the chapter, here is what we've learned:

◆ Three important elements of membership sites are customer value proposition, sustainability, and timing

◆ Blocking access to posts in a specific category based on a membership level

◆ How to take advantage of cross-promoting social networking sites, while simultaneously outlining the benefits of your site on a **Members Option Page**

◆ Implementing page-specific custom CSS and JavaScript

◆ Advantages of S2 Member and CubePoints

With each chapter introducing you to new avenues in growing your site and spurring more activity, it becomes increasingly difficult to figure out what works and what doesn't. In the next chapter, you'll learn how to use certain metrics and measure results to fine-tune your site.

5
Keeping Up with the Stats

More than two billion worldwide Internet users, or more than a quarter of the world population, spent 2.9 billion hours on YouTube in 2011. About 25 billion tweets were sent on Twitter, a quarter billion of Internet users signed up on Facebook, and a total of 176 million blogs populate the Internet. Two sentences ago, you probably never knew these impressive facts, but all of this data is derived through analytics.

In the previous chapters, we learned how to engage visitors on our site by building memberships, social networks, and sending out newsletters. In this chapter, we're going to switch gears by learning some basic web analytics implementations, gauge our social engagement efforts, what they mean and how to report them.

Here's what's in store for the next several pages:

- The big deal behind hits versus pageviews
- Defining absolute unique visitors, bounce rates, and conversion rates
- Tracking links (campaigns) through Google Analytics and bitly
- Comparing traffic between two time periods
- Automatically sending analytical PDF reports through e-mail

There is a lot to uncover in this chapter, so grab your favourite beverage and let's begin.

Understanding key terminology

In the early 1990s when the majority of web geeks were using words such as *hits* to describe pageviews, Webalizer and AWStats were two of the popular applications to gauge web traffic. While their respective reports looked relatively primitive, these web log analysers provided a decent amount of information to report the most frequently accessed entry and exit pages, among other data. Then, in 2005, Google acquired Urchin Analytics and provided enterprise-level analytics software to the masses for free. Now, under the veil of **Google Analytics (GA)**, it's standard practice to deploy GA on every website imaginable. It's for this reason that we expect to see granular data and use key terms such as **absolute unique visitors**, **bounce rates**, and **conversion rates**, when describing site activity. While this may be the first time you see some of these terms, it's important to know them for context.

When a traffic collision occurs on the road and you call the police, the dispatch will ask you several questions. When and where did the collision occur, or what is the current condition of the victim? Answers to these questions provide a point of reference to the dispatch to assist the victim. Details such as street names, crossroads, or bodily injuries are all essential pieces of information. The same is true for the technical jargon that's involved when it comes to your website. It's extremely difficult to troubleshoot an aspect of your site, if you cannot properly define the issue. So let's get on with the analytics lingo.

Pageviews versus hits

In most cases, it's inaccurate to use *hits* to describe pageviews. That's because a *hit* refers to the amount of visitor requests to the server to fetch data. However, almost all webpages need multiple server requests for images, scripts, CSS, and other files. For example, a page with two images and some text would translate into three hits—one request to load the page with the text, one request for the first image, and one request for the second image. A **pageview**, on the other hand, means exactly what it implies—viewing or visiting a page one time. Taking the previous example, a visitor can be tracked with one pageview, but this single visit could break down into three hits.

Absolute unique visitors versus unique pageviews

When you're in a business setting and discussing analytics regarding your site, you will most likely hear the term *unique* thrown left and right. Generally, while this may refer to unique pageviews, it's often referring to your **absolute unique visitors**. Unique, by definition, means one of a kind. In the analytics realm, a **unique pageview** is a visit to one of your pages by the same user when visiting the site again typically within the same day. In comparison, a normal pageview also counts page refreshes as additional pageviews. If a visitor leaves your page and then returns to the same page, this is also counted as another pageview, hence, making this figure less accurate.

Absolute unique visitors are different from unique pageviews in that you're recording the number of users, not their actions. In GA, absolute unique visitors are essentially new, first-time visitors to your website who will not be counted in subsequent visits. This is a key metric because a site with 500 absolute unique visitors has more of an advantage over a site that reports 500 unique pageviews, for example. Unlike the former, a large amount of unique pageviews can mean a lot of engagement, but it does not guarantee more visitors. In fact, you may find it challenging to increase the amount of unique visitors. Having a large user-base, or absolute unique visitors, though, means you can tweak your content to get more unique pageviews out of your existing visitors; your starting point is more advantageous.

Bounce rates and conversion rates

If you've ever been in the position to have a web developer, marketer, or consultant review your site traffic, chances are he or she mentioned bounce and conversion rates. These are, perhaps, the two most important metrics next to absolute unique visitors, when analysing site data. Specifically, they refer to user engagement. Bounce rate refers to the percentage of visitors who leave your page upon arriving to it. Think of it in terms of channel surfing. Sometimes, when you flip through television channels, it'll only take you a second to switch to the next program. Sometimes, the moment you turn on the TV, there's something you'll want to see. It all depends on the relevancy of the content at hand. When referring to your website, the higher the relevancy of your content, the lower the chances are of your visitors leaving your page, which equates to a lower bounce rate. Conversely, a site that has a high bounce rate measuring at 75 percent, for example, is irrelevant to three out of four people visiting your page.

A conversion rate, in its most basic form, is the percentage used to measure the ratio of people converting from one state into another. In marketing terms, this usually means the ratio of prospective customers converting into buyers. In GA, a conversion rate is a bit more specific, because it's based on goals. If you set up a simple sign-up page on your site and define it as a goal, GA will measure the conversion for visitors who visit that page and complete the signup. They have effectively converted from being visitors into being subscribers, buyers, or whatever else you're trying to convert them to. It's closely tied to the bounce rate, because the lower the bounce rate, the higher the conversion rate. Again, it's another powerful metric that gives you some insight into the engagement of your content.

Creating a Google Analytics account and tracking your site

All the social media marketing methods described in this book are measurable. In most cases, it's fairly quick and easy to track them, as well. The following are some quick guides on how to set up and measure your efforts.

Time for Action – the quick guide to implementing analytics for your site

There are multiple ways to add GA to your site; however, this is one of the most effective and fastest ways to get going:

1. Log on to `https://accounts.google.com/NewAccount` and create a new Google account, if you don't have one already.

2. Once signed into your account, log on to `http://www.google.com/analytics/` and click on the **Access Analytics** button to log into GA.

3. In the orange header, click on the **Admin** link toward the right and then press the **+ New Account** button to create your tracking code for your site, as shown in the following screenshot:

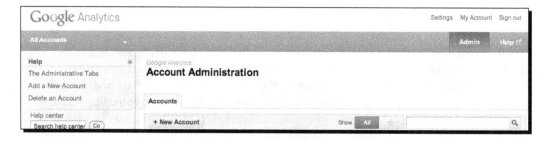

4. Continue onto the next page by providing an **Account Name**, **Website's URL**, **Time zone**, accept the **Terms and conditions**, and click on **Create Account** button to receive your tracking code, as show in the following screenshot:

5. Your tracking code will be located toward the bottom of the page under the header labeled **Paste this code on your site**. This is a JavaScript snippet that you could manually paste into your site. However, since we'll be using a plugin to automatically do this for us, we're only interested in the the portion of the code that looks like this UA-89096216-1, which is your Google Analytics site tracking ID. Write this down, since you might need it later.

6. Next, in your WordPress dashboard, navigate to **Add New** under **Plugins** and search for **Google Analytics for WordPress** by **Joost de Valk**. Install and activate the plugin.

7. To add the GA tracking code to your entire site, navigate to **Google Analytics** under **Settings**. In the **Analytics Profile**, press the **Click here to authenticate with Google** button and press the **Grant access** button on the next page, as shown in the following screenshot. Select the appropriate accounts for the **Account and Profile** drop-down selections. Alternatively, if you only see a blank field next to the **Analytics Profile** label, enter your GA user ID from Step 5. Remember to press the **Update Google Analytics Settings** button to save your changes.

8. To get more granular analytics data, you may chose to log other variables under the **Custom Variables Settings** section.

9. Under **Advanced Settings**, select **Administrator for Ignore users**, so you don't inflate your data each time you visit your own site, unless you don't have enough data for testing. Also be sure to select the option for **Add tracking to the login and registration forms** to receive that data, as well:

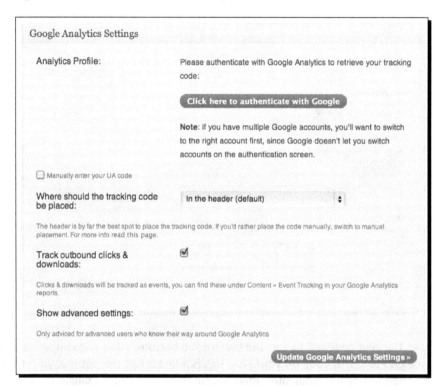

What just happened?

Google Analytics has become the golden standard for tracking site statistics, so we registered for a free account to take advantage of this service. Then, we created a GA profile to receive a site-specific tracking code. As WordPress doesn't natively come with GA tracking enabled, we downloaded a plugin to globally add the tracking code to our site.

Now that we have the basic tracking enabled, we'll take it up a notch in the next activity by tracking our social media marketing campaigns to measure the effectiveness. This will give us a good gauge to understand if those efforts reach our audience, as we'll be able to see if our visitors and Twitter followers are interested in our content. If they are, we'll see those statistics (that is, the number of visits and related data) in our GA account. Let's continue.

Time for action – tracking a tweet to your site through Google Analytics

Before you start this activity, be sure to have the link to the page you want to promote handy. You may have it ready to go, if you've pasted the URL into your clipboard. Alternatively, just start a new browser session and keep the promotional page open in another window.

1. Bookmark and log on to Google's URL Builder page at `http://www.google.com/support/analytics/bin/answer.py?hl=en&answer=55578`.

2. Enter the link to the page you want to promote in the **Website URL** field.

3. Continue by entering `twitter` under the **Campaign Source**, since you'll be pointing your Twitter followers through that site. Enter `tweet` under **Campaign Medium**, as that is the method with which you promote your page. Last, give this promotion a name under **Campaign Name**. For example, if you're launching your site, give it a name of `launch`, as shown in the following screenshot:

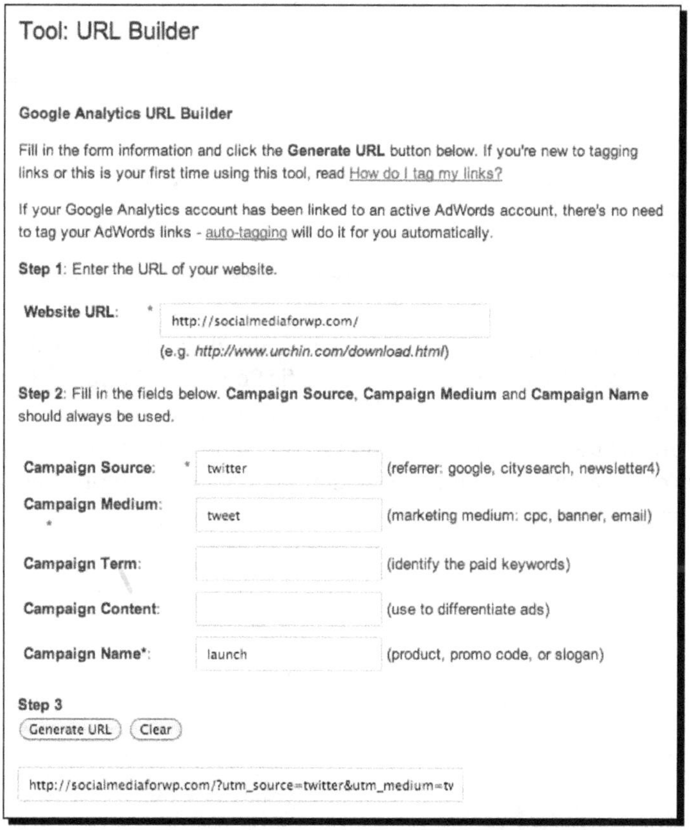

4. Press the **Generate URL** button, which will generate a long link that's sure to take up most of your 140-character limit on Twitter. Write it down or copy it to your clipboard as you'll need it for the next step.

5. Create a free bitly account by logging on to `http://bitly.com` and enter your link from Step 4 in the big field that reads **Shorten your links and share from here**, once you're logged in.

6. The bitly service will automatically create a new, shorter link for you, but we'll improve it a bit. Click on the **Customize** link and give it a better display name like `2012launch` or anything similar that's available.

7. From here, you can click on the **Twitter Sign In** button to tweet, which will point you to a Twitter authorization page, connecting bitly with Twitter. Once connected, you can create your post or tweet using the **Share** button, as show in the following screenshot. Alternatively, you can copy and paste the bitly link from Step 6 and use it within Twitter itself:

8. To view your campaigns in Google Analytics, simply log into your GA dashboard, navigate to your site and then click on **Traffic Sources | Sources | Campaigns** in the left sidebar. Your campaign data should be visible after 24 hours. You can even filter, or drill down your content by how much time your visitors spent on your campaign page by clicking on the drop-down selection under the **Explorer** tab, as shown in the following screenshot:

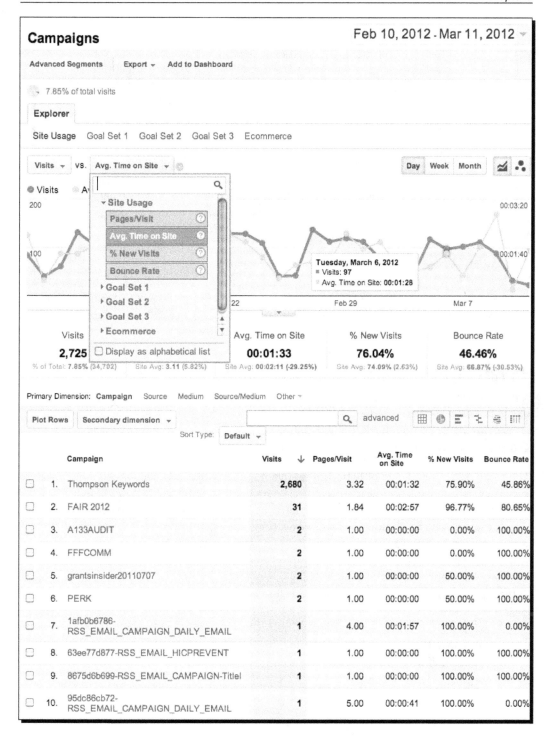

bitly

There are a handful of URL shortening services, but bitly is by far one of the most popular ones. The main advantage of using this service is that clicks to your bitly link are tracked in real-time, which you can see once you're logged into your bitly account. The integration into Twitter also saves you time in posting your tweets. If you want to read more about bitly and its capabilities, visit `http://bitly.com/pages/help`.

You can take the implementation for bitly a step further by implementing it for the activity outlined in *Part 2: Creating tweets through forum content* of *Chapter 3*. Simply go to **WP to Twitter** under **Settings** and select bitly from the **Choose your short URL service** drop-down selection, after you enter your bitly login credentials in the **URL Shortener Account Settings** section.

What just happened?

You learned how to track links from an outbound referrer such as Twitter back to your site, using a third-party URL shortening service—bitly and Google's own URL Builder. This included utilizing an easy-to-remember display name through bitly, after you created a campaign name, source, and medium for your traceable link.

Reporting data with Google Analytics, bitly and Twitter

A full, accurate overview of your site's data using Google Analytics takes 24 hours, meaning you will always be an entire day behind when you review and report data. In contrast, bitly is great for giving you real-time statistics when people click on your link, which is useful for gauging their interest in your content. Unfortunately, you're limited to only this metric.

The combination of GA and bitly becomes advantageous when you plan ahead and strategize campaigns around your content. This doesn't mean you need to create a full-blown campaign rife with Google AdWords, promotional giveaways, or e-mail drip campaigns. It simply means you should think of several key items you want to promote throughout the week, be it on Twitter, Facebook, or any other social network. Of course, there will be times when the ebb and flow of your content will become somewhat stagnant, so you should not feel obligated to track every single thing you want to promote 100 percent of the time. Suffice to say, track your tweets or any other link when one or all of the following apply:

- The content you're promoting warrants the time and effort to track
- You have the time and energy to analyze your data and apply changes to your site or content, if need be
- You need to prove or measure the effectiveness of your campaign or content

GA's set of data gets so granular that you can easily get lost in the numbers. Don't worry, the next half of this chapter will help you understand some of the key aspects you want to focus on. If you want to know how else you can apply what you've learned so far in this quick guide to analytics, take note of the next section, which delves into campaign tracking.

The gold mine of campaign tracking

You've learned how to track a tweet, using the quick guide in this chapter, but what's more important is that you've gone through the actual steps to create a campaign, which is traceable. Using the steps outlined in the activity, you can also apply campaign tracking not only for tweets but also for the following:

◆ Links in e-mails or newsletters

◆ Links pointing to special landing pages (for example, promotional pages)

◆ Links posted in other social networks such as Facebook, LinkedIn, or Google+

◆ Links printed on print material (for example, promotional posters)

The information you collect from these special links or URL campaigns, provide provides invaluable insight as how to shape your content to maximize visitor interest and interaction. Following the pop quiz, we'll go over exactly how to read the information you've extracted.

Pop quiz – the quick guide to analytics

1. Hits are accurate metrics for site traffic.

    a. True

    b. False

2. Bounce rate refers to the percentage of visitors who leave your page upon arriving at it.

    a. True

    b. False

3. Unique pageviews are more accurate than regular pageviews in Google Analytics.

    a. True

    b. False

4. Google's URL Builder is a useful URL shortening service.

    a. True

    b. False

5. It takes 24 hours for a full, accurate set of data to appear in Google Analytics.

    a.   True

    b.   False

Reviewing and reporting analytics

In the first half of the chapter, you learned some key terminology to better describe what's happening on your site. This second half will go over what happens, after you've captured all that data. Specifically, you'll learn how to navigate within Google Analytics to make sense of your site's traffic including bounce rates, absolute unique visitors, pageviews, campaigns, and more. Luckily, reading your site's traffic is even easier than implementing tracking code to your site and links.

Comparing traffic from one week to another week

Google Analytics provides lots of resources within the reports themselves, offering you advice and activities. You may find yourself figuring out even more advanced topics when it comes to GA and its tracking capabilities. The following activities are just meant as a primer to get you started.

Time for action – the quick guide to reading analytics

A common practice of reviewing data is that of a comparison from one time period to another. By default, GA displays all traffic within a one-month period up to the current day. In the following example, we'll narrow the analytics down to a week and compare it with another week, starting with absolute unique visitors traffic:

1. In your GA dashboard, navigate to the bold **Audience** link off the left-side menu and click on **Overview**.

2. In the large date field for you data, located near the top right of the page, click on the arrow that's pointing downward to display more options.

3. The following screenshot displays a one-week date range starting with **November 3, 2010**. To select your own date range, use the date picker and click on the start date to begin your date range and then click on the same day a week later to end your date range. Alternatively, you can enter the date manually in the date fields adjacent to the date picker:

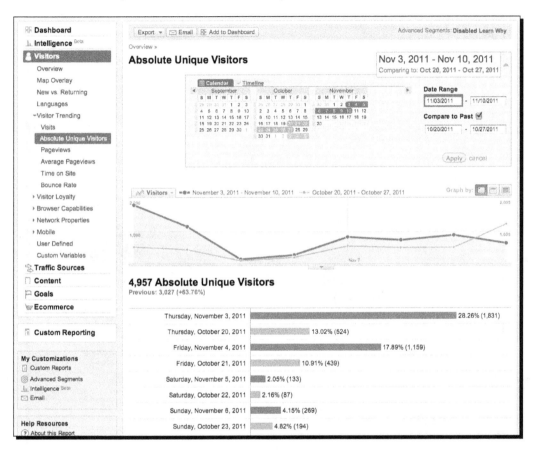

4. To compare this date range with another, check the box labeled **Compare to Past**, which will display another start-and-end date field. By default, GA will select the last four weeks for your date range from Step 3. However, the second date range, that is the comparison, will be offset by default. To get a more accurate comparison, we'll change this range by starting the one-week comparison on the same day. In this example, that day is *Thursday*. Simply change the date fields to get the *Thursday-to-Thursday* comparison, using the date picker or entering the new dates manually like you did in the previous step. Both date ranges should be reflected in green and blue colors.

5. The number of absolute unique visitors for your first date range will be presented in big bold letters under the line graph. If you want to find out the difference of new visits gained or lost during this time period, select the **% New Visits** option from the drop-down selection under the **Overview** tab, as shown in the following screenshot. You can also select the **Bounce Rate** or **Unique Visitors** for a different comparison:

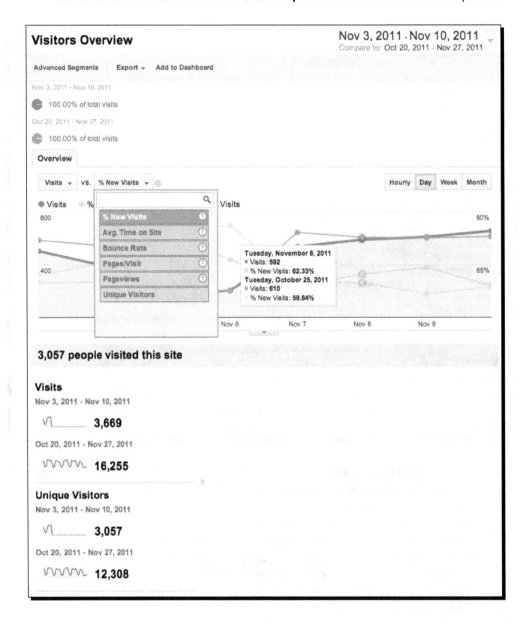

6. If you have to report certain data to anyone, you can send reports to them through e-mail. However, you'll have to use the previous version of Google Analytics by clicking on the **Old Version** link toward the top-right corner next to your Gmail address. Once you've navigated to your site overview, click on the **Email** button in the gray bar toward the top of the page near the report title. PDFs make for the most e-mail and reader-friendly formats, which you can select under **Format**, as shown in the screenshot. Fill out the remaining fields and finish by clicking on the **Send** button:

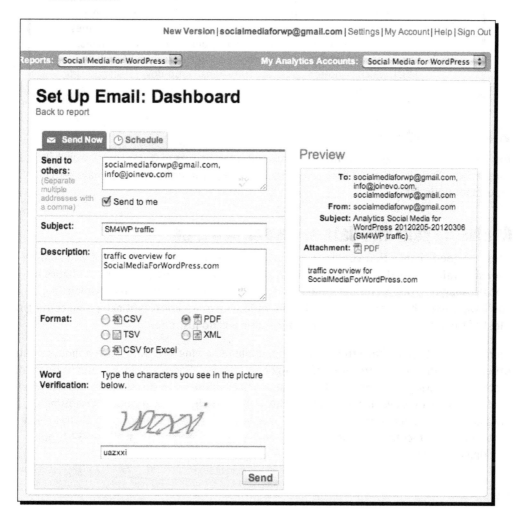

7. You can automate e-mailed PDF reports by clicking on the **Schedule** tab and entering e-mail addresses in the **Send to others** field. The default frequency is per week, which you can change by selecting a different value from the **Date Range/Schedule** drop-down selection. Be sure to clear your date range values before proceeding and uncheck the **Include date comparison** checkbox, as you'll most likely want to provide simple snapshots of your traffic, not comparisons with a specific date ranges.

A lot of the times when you want to compare fiscal quarters from one quarter to the next, the extended date ranges will make your line graph look like a seismic wave full of ups and downs. This data is sometimes better visualized using weekly or monthly units. To change the units, simply press either one of the two icons listed next to the **Graph by** label, which is located under the **Date Range** drop-down selection near the top right.

What just happened?

You learned how to segment traffic data into two specific sets in order to draw an A/B comparison. You also learned how to change the line graph units and automate e-mail reports for your data.

Analysing your site data one week at a time

There's a good chance that you'll easily grow tired and, perhaps, frustrated if you analyze your site traffic every day. While day-to-day comparisons are just as easy to configure in Google Analytics, this is cumbersome and not very efficient. In fact, the only plausible time you'll want to do it is when you've got a site re-launch or an important campaign coming up. Most of the time, a weekly analysis of your traffic will do just fine.

Important facets you'll have to bear in mind, while reviewing site traffic, are holidays or any other significant days where site traffic might be affected. For example, you might encounter more traffic during the winter and spring seasons as opposed to the summer season when a lot of people are travelling, not surfing the web. If you find your numbers discouraging, always check for outside factors that may have led to the decline. Above all, always check that your site is recording traffic. If you see zero pageviews, chances are your GA is not tracking properly.

Have a go hero

In this chapter, you learned how to harness the power of Google Analytics to measure the traffic to your site. If you've never measured your site data, this is the perfect opportunity for you to understand your visitors and their interests. Based on the activities outlined in this chapter, can you turn any of your upcoming promotions into campaigns that you can track through GA? Are there any automated e-mail campaigns you've created in *Chapter 1, Share it the Easy Way* that you can measure? What if you could track all of your site members' BuddyPress Achievements? How valuable is that data to you, and how would you take advantage of it to improve your content? Almost everything is measurable. What you make out of the data and how you apply it is how it will affect you the most, so start scratching your head for the most essential piece of information you need to know about your users.

Summary

In addition to learning a brief history to web statistics, this chapter introduced you to some key terminology, so you're able to properly describe what's happening on your site. You also learned about key metrics to provide you with some context for visitors and pageviews. Along the way, you discovered the following:

- How to trace a tweet and other links in Google Analytics
- How and where to access time-segmented data in GA
- E-mail automation for analytical reports
- A few tips to help you improve the visualization of your data when dealing with a long date range

In the next chapter, you'll learn how you can leverage this newfound data to improve your site, as you'll learn how to manage your site. You'll learn how to react to your site users, both in terms of support and site logistics.

6

Managing your Site

It seemed as though 2011 marked the year of technology outages for some of the world's most reputable companies. The Sony PlayStation Network was hacked twice, resulting in 93,000 account suspensions, 70 million BlackBerry users experienced a three-day e-mail and Internet blackout,, and www.WordPress.com *came under a denial-of-service (DoS) attack—the largest in its history, which affected nearly 18 million popular blogs, including CNN and TechCrunch. While it's certainly difficult to anticipate problems of this magnitude, contingency plans can make all the difference when experiencing downtime.*

We learned the significance of measuring site statistics in the last chapter for your social media efforts. Site maintenance is no different. A well-managed site is as important as a well thought-out social media marketing campaign. It's essential to your credibility and reputation. Here's what we'll learn in this chapter:

- ◆ Three aspects of maintenance and how to approach each one
- ◆ A lesson learned through Facebook's Beacon
- ◆ The truth about 99 percent server availability
- ◆ How to prepare and recover from server downtime
- ◆ How to automatically backup your site and store information to a cloud service
- ◆ 10 free plugins to help you manage your site
- ◆ How to publish posts through e-mail

Let's dive in.

Damage control—key aspects of maintenance

Managing your site can translate into different responsibilities, depending on whom you talk to. They can usually be grouped into three categories:

- **Hardware**: your live server, development server, **Content Delivery Networks** (**CDN**), cloud services, caching settings, database optimization, and so on
- **Software**:WordPress plugin and theme updates, content backups, any third-party services tied to your site(s)
- **Site Users**: spam prevention, user feedback, site-related troubleshooting, and so on

When to use a dedicated server

Assuming that you're starting out with a low-traffic website (a few hundred unique visitors a month), you will most likely not run into any issues when it comes to running your site on a cheap server. However, once traffic starts to pick up, one of two things will happen:

- Your website will time out with some sort of *member exceeded bandwidth limit* page or message that will leave your visitors utterly perplexed
- Your visitors will complain that your site takes forever and a day to load, making for a horrible user experience, which may lead to a stunted growth in traffic.

You'll probably get several e-mail notifications regarding site errors, in all likelihood, but the key is to prevent this from occurring in the first place. While this isn't a book about server specialization, specifications, or modifications, there is a general rule of thumb. You will need a dedicated server if you anticipate any of the following:

- You're going to run a membership-based site (that is, BuddyPress, WP Symposium, or any other type of site where you'll have an ample amount of users clicking on multiple pages during the same session)
- You're running a network of sites using multi-site (formerly known as WPMU)
- You're going to have a high-traffic site centered on message boards (that is, support forums or any general forum where you need snappy loading times)
- Your traffic is growing at an exponential rate, much faster than you anticipated in the weeks leading up to the surge

Running a dedicated server means everything will load fast every time, enabling all of your users to engage with each other without any hassles. The last thing people want to do is wait ten seconds for a page to load, so that they can share it with friends or colleagues on Twitter or any other social networking site. In most cases, once you have everything configured, including any CDNs or other cloud services, managing it becomes relatively quick and easy. Unfortunately, dedicated servers and cloud services can become expensive, so you should always do your research before committing to a webhost.

When to upgrade WordPress and your plugins

Automatic software upgrades have become almost standard. Google's web browser, Chrome, for example, downloads updates in the background and applies them upon the next launch. This isn't the case with WordPress. Sure, the system will notify you of recommended updates, but you still have to be proactive about actually upgrading the platform. Otherwise, you'll likely experience software vulnerabilities or security breaches. The same goes for themes and plugins. Update WordPress and all of its extensions. If you're unsure whether anything will break, you can always perform a test upgrade on your development server whenever they become available.

Along with WP-related updates comes your content, which needs maintenance, as well. Specifically speaking, you will want daily backups that include your posts, images, and any other files associated with your WP-powered site. Here's why—let's assume your site gets hacked and all of your Twitter followers and Facebook fans start to complain online. If you don't know that your site was hacked two days prior to everyone's complaints, and you keep backups that only go back one day, you'll be in a lot of trouble when you try to restore your site. The simplest and most effective backup solution is Automattic's own backup service in the form of a plugin called **VaultPress**, which provides real-time backups for all of your sites (even multi-sites). It is a paid service, though, so we'll go over a free alternative solution in the upcoming activity. Much like managing the hardware portion of your site, managing software is relatively simple.

How to manage your site users

A **site user** is a blanket term for a visitor, member, administrator, and anybody else that accesses or uses your site. Managing one user is easy; managing a horde of online users is extremely challenging. If you remove a feature or your site loads too slow, your users will let you know in droves. Keeping them satisfied essentially translates into easing them to changes. Failure to do so can result in a massive public relations mess and class action lawsuit, as was the case with Facebook's Beacon, the controversial advertising program that was shut down in late 2009, which published certain information without users' explicit permission when it first launched. Case in point—be transparent, upfront, and honest about your intentions.

You're doing it wrong is a popular remark used throughout the blogosphere and typically comes with the assumption that a user has failed to perform an action properly. It's a brusque and otherwise unwelcoming response that you, as a site administrator, undoubtedly thought about telling your users at one point. But much to the dismay that can result after hurling those words at people who took the initiative to participate on your site, it's best to err on the side of caution. Remain courteous, respectful, and welcome constructive criticism in any form. Hardware and software malfunctions are easy to fix in comparison to people and relationships, no thanks to the permanence of the web.

Time for action – how to create automated daily backups for your site

Multiple WordPress plugins exist on the repository to create backups for your site, but the majority of them do not back up your entire site's directory and most of them also do not store them to another location. The following will show you how to achieve both, so let's get started:

1. Log on to `https://www.dropbox.com/register` to create your free dropbox account, which will let you store up to 2 gigabytes (GB) of data onto the cloud server.

2. Next, in your WordPress Dashboard, navigate to **Add New** under **Plugins** and search for **WordPress Backup to Dropbox**. Install and activate the plugin.

3. In order to connect your WordPress site with Dropbox, you'll have to navigate to **Backup to Dropbox** under **Settings** and link your account. Simply press the **Authorize** button, which will prompt you to log into your dropbox account, if you're not logged in already. You may be asked to confirm your authentication, which you will need to approve to link your account, so press the **Allow** button.

4. Back in WordPress, click on the **Continue** button to complete all the backup settings. The plugin will try to create a backup folder on your server to store your database (`.sql`) backup for your site. If it's not successful, you may need to create the directory manually using an FTP client such as, FileZilla. This directory will also need to be writeable by your server, so you will most likely want to use the `755` chmod, which is a permission setting for your server to write on selected files and folders.

5. Next, you can adjust the **Day**, **Time**, and **Frequency** of your backups, using the drop-down selections. It's best to pick a time when you have a very low amount of traffic and everything has been posted. If you're unsure leave default midnight settings and change the **Frequency** to **Daily**. Be sure to press the **Save Changes** button to update your settings.

6. At this point, you're set up for with your automated backups. If you want, you can manually start your first backup by clicking on the **Backup now** link next to the **Save Changes** button. To access any of your backed up files, you can use your native dropbox application on your computer, or you can access your account online.

7. If you ever want to revert to an earlier version of any file, log onto your online account, which should bring you to the **Files** section, indicated by the highlighted tab near the top. Click on the **WordPressBackup** directory to reveal your backed up files. To revert to an earlier version of your theme's index.php file, for example, navigate to your theme under the **themes** directory within the **wp-content** directory. Use the checkbox to select which files you want to revert. Click on the highlighted portion to reveal more options (context menu), then click on the **Previous versions** link, make your selection, and click on the **Restore** button.

8. Finally, you may want to create a disclaimer page on your WordPress site, which will say that your company is not liable for any lost data:

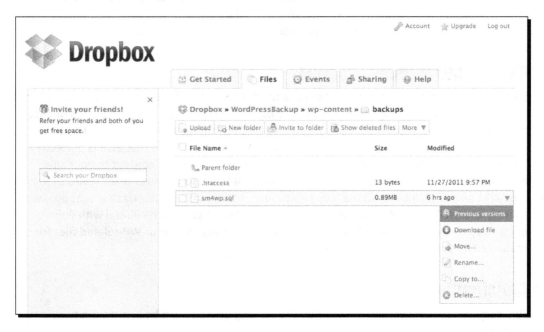

Backup Alternative: XCloner

XCloner is another free alternative site backup and restore plugin. It's more granular in that you can specify the directories you'd like to back up. Backups can be automatically stored on your server, transferred to another server through FTP or sent directly to Amazon's S3 cloud storage. All backups are compressed, so you can easily download and store them manually on dropbox, as well. XCloner offers multiple support services, depending on your budget. More information on this plugin can be found at http://www.xcloner.com.

What just happened?

Creating automated backups to Dropbox first required you to register with a free account, which enabled you to upload 2 GB of online storage. Then, you proceeded with an authentication process to connect your WordPress site with dropbox. Finally, you configured the backup plugin to automatically send backups to Dropbox on a daily basis. You also learned how to revert to an older version of a backed up file, and you were introduced to an alternative backup system that stores your files to Amazon's cloud service.

Advantages of using Dropbox

Like the other reputable services and plugins used throughout this book, Dropbox provides reliable web hosting, going strong with a user-base of 45 million people. While 2GB of data may not seem a lot, you'll most likely be able to take advantage of the free level for the first several months, if your site is relatively small. You may even find that 2GB is perfectly adequate to suit your needs, if you find yourself not posting a lot of content to your site. However, if you start to accumulate a lot of data, Dropbox also provides three levels of paid upgrades as well as mobile access to your account. Additionally, its interface is snappy, user-friendly, and makes file sharing simple. Bear in mind that if you can be liberal with your budget, you may want to use VaultPress instead, as it scans all of your WP-related files for malware and provides security notifications.

Anticipating downtime

Two common misconceptions among novices starting up a site can be summarized as follows:

◆ First, social media means throwing a bunch of Facebook, Twitter, or LinkedIn badges on your site and letting your users do the rest

◆ Second, the hardware (that is, your server), doesn't have a huge impact on your site and backup software is non-essential when you first roll out your site

When it comes to server availability, you'll at least want to be aware of the fact that it will go down, no matter how much you pay. To give you an idea of the actual amount of downtime you'll experience, look no further than the following chart, which gives estimates of some of the most commonly advertised server availabilities:

Availability %	Downtime per year	Downtime per month	Downtime per week
99%	3.65 days	7.20 hours	1.68 hours
99.9%	8.76 hours	43.2 minutes	10.1 minutes
99.99%	52.56 minutes	4.32 minutes	1.01 minutes
99.999%	5.26 minutes	25.9 seconds	6.05 seconds
99.9999%	31.5 seconds	2.59 seconds	0.605 seconds

Most times when you encounter downtime because of your web host, you'll be up and running within the hour. But when your site goes down because of malicious code and you anticipate several hours of downtime, while you troubleshoot the issue, you'll be glad you've completed all the steps that enabled you to automate your daily backups to restore your site.

The upsell during downtime

When your site goes down, you might be lucky enough that it happens at some odd time, like on the stroke of midnight, when everyone is tucked up in bed. If you're even luckier, you'll have your IT department troubleshoot the issue for you in a short amount of time. But for those other instances when downtime occurs in the middle of your day, here's how you can turn panic into profit—limited-time discounts. During downtime, a common practice for site managers is to put up a **splash page**, which points all pages of the site to a central page that states something along the lines of *The page you're trying to access is temporarily unavailable, because of site maintenance*. However, if you happen to sell any products or services on your site, this is the perfect opportunity to apologize to your site visitors for the downtime by supplying them with discount codes instead. A useful plugin to accomplish this is called **WP Maintenance Mode**, which allows you to create your own custom html page. You can drop in Gravity Forms, MailChimp forms, or any other lead-capture forms to e-mail discounts or other offers, as well, to convert the frustration you've caused your users. However, if you do not have access to your WordPress Dashboard and enough space on your server to display your special offer page, be sure to try your other social media networking outlets such as Facebook, Twitter or YouTube.

If you can't offer any discounts, while your site experiences technical difficulties, try to entertain your users instead. One of the web's most famous, or infamous, yet beloved pages is the fail whale page that Twitter uses, whenever the service is unavailable. Over the years, it has gotten so popular through social media, no less that you can even purchase fail whale merchandise.

Pop quiz – WordPress maintenance

1. Three key aspects to WordPress maintenance are Beacon, BuddyPress and Boxdrop.

    a. True

    b. False

2. A site user is a blanket term for a visitor, member, administrator, and anybody else that accesses or uses your site.

    a. True

    b. False

3. You should back up your site on a daily basis.

    a. True

    b. False

4. You can experience more than 40 minutes of downtime with 99.9 percent server availability.

    a. True

    b. False

5. You should set your permission bits to 644 when creating your backup folder.

    a. True

    b. False

Getting organized and managing time

This book deals extensively with automating processes because social media revolves around good content, as echoed throughout previous chapters, and, creating good content on a continuous basis is a laborious process. Once you've found your rhythm on producing or curating meaningful content that others would want to talk about, then you've moved on to managing your site. Oftentimes, this means managing other content producers (editors, authors, or contributors), if you've graduated to enlisting new staff members to help you churn out the material. While it's fine to keep doing everything the same way as you did initially, there is room for improvement. Following is a collection of useful plugins to help you stay organized, so you can spend less time on mundane tasks and spend more time managing and strategizing your content.

Top ten free plugins to help you run your site efficiently

Aside from the plugins that you should be using already, such as Google XML Sitemaps and Akismet, there are a good handful of plugins lurking in the WordPress repository that will make your life, as a site manager, easier. Here's a roundup of ten of the best free ones:

1. **Editorial Calendar**: When you have multiple authors producing content for your site, keeping a track of scheduled posts can become fairly monotonous. This powerful calendar plugin provides you with a bird's eye view of all your content. Learn more at `http://wordpress.org/extend/plugins/editorial-calendar`.

2. **Edit Flow**: By default, WordPress only supports three statuses for publishing posts (Published, Pending Review, and Draft). Edit Flow not only allows you to create more post statuses, but it also enables you to enter editorial metadata such as, due dates, required word count, assigned photographers, and more. It also provides you with a simple workflow to create user and group notification subscriptions for editorial members. Learn more at `http://editflow.org`.

3. **WordPress Backup to Dropbox**: You've already learned how to utilize this plugin in this chapter's activity. It's a great alternative to VaultPress, as well, and if you'd rather use Amazon's S3 cloud storage, you can use Xcloner instead. Learn more at `http://www.mikeyd.com.au/projects/wordpress-backup-to-dropbox/` and `http://www.xcloner.com`.

4. **AutoChimp**: This is useful to complement the MailChimp activity outlined in Chapter 1. It makes e-mail campaigns, using category-specific posts more manageable, as you don't have to access the MailChimp site. Learn more at `http://www.wandererllc.com/company/plugins/autochimp`.

5. **Twitter Blackbird Pie**: The process of referencing your Twitter followers within a post is tedious. The attribution usually calls for the Twitter name, tweet, and time stamp, which you'd have to copy and paste individually. This plugin allows you to reference the tweets by URLs or IDs and produces a pretty pullout quote, which site visitors can then retweet, mark as favorite or reply to. Learn more at `http://wordpress.org/extend/plugins/twitter-blackbird-pie`.

6. **Jetpack** (WordPress.com Stats): There is no web statistics software more powerful than Google Analytics that's free. However, logging into Google Analytics every day and clicking through all the reports can become unproductive at times. With Jetpack, you'll gain access to WordPress Statistics, which will give you an analytics section within your WordPress Dashboard. Jetpack also ships with the aforementioned plugin After the Deadline, it requires a free registration at WordPress.com. Learn more at `http://jetpack.me`.

7. **Usernoise modal feedback/contact form**: When you launch, re-launch, or add new features to your site, you'll most likely want to collect feedback. This plugin adds a little **feedback** tab to the side of your site, which displays a pop-up box where visitors can provide their comments. Feedback is automatically sent to your inbox, providing you with real-time updates, while also storing it as a custom post type in your Dashboard. A paid pro version is also available, which adds more features such as feedback lists and discussions. Learn more at `http://wordpress.org/extend/plugins/usernoise`.

8. **Broken Link Checker**: It's common to forget fixing broken links. It's grunt work. But if you care about usability and search engine optimization, you'll want to install and activate this simple plugin, which regularly scans your site and notifies you of broken links through e-mail. Learn more at `http://wordpress.org/extend/plugins/broken-link-checker`.

9. **WP Maintenance Mode**: The WordPress repository is home to several maintenance-type plugins, but this one leads the pack by allowing you to go as simple as displaying a message with a countdown timer or allowing you to customize the whole page completely, using your own custom stylesheet. Learn more at `http://wordpress.org/extend/plugins/wp-maintenance-mode`.

10. **Collabpress**: Devising strategies such as running limited-time member promotions, as outlined in Chapter 4, *VIP Memberships*, requires organizational planning. Collabpress is a turnkey solution that enables a project management layer on top of your WordPress site. With this tool, you'll be able to assign team members to a project and assign tasks for all of your social media campaigns. Learn more at `http://collabpress.org`.

Lowering the barrier of writing

Sometimes, the easiest task can become a huge burden. For example, when you publish a post through WordPress, you first have to launch your browser, navigate to your WordPress site, log in, create a new post, then write it, and then publish it. The mere thought of going through these motions may be reason enough for you to get discouraged from writing original content. As this is what we want to avoid, we'll learn of a quicker and simpler way to get your posts published through your site. All it requires, after you've completed the activity, is knowing how to write an e-mail. Surely, that's simple enough.

Time for action – how to write and automatically publish posts through e-mail

If there is one more way to simplify the workload associated with publishing posts to your site using WordPress, it's publishing through your site through e-mail. WordPress provides post-by-e-mail functions natively. However, it's laborious to set up, if you can get it working. Hence, we'll get you up and running in no time, using a third-party service called Posterous that specializes in this one task and simplifies everything to make your life less stressful:

1. Log on to `https://posterous.com/register` and register for a free account.

2. Next, check your e-mail for an e-mail confirmation message from **Posterous** and press the **Confirm Email** button. If you do not receive the e-mail right away, be sure to check your spam folder and allow e-mails to come from `no-reply@posterous.com`.

3. Once signed in, click on the **Manage Spaces** link in the left sidebar and click on the name of your space, located under **Your Spaces**. Notice that the boxed menu items to the right will change.

4. Click on **Autopost Setup** under **Posts** in the boxed menu items to the right. Then, click on the large **+ Add a service** button to connect your WordPress site with Posterous. Upon clicking the button, you will be presented with a large list of services that you can connect with; press the **WordPress** option. This will lead to the next step, as shown in the following screenshot.

5. When you're asked to provide information to **Link Your Meta Weblog Account**, provide the URL of your address with a working set of username and password credentials to connect your site. (You may be asked to log into your WordPress site to enable this step by logging into your WordPress Dashboard, navigating to **Writing** under **Settings** and checking **Enable the WordPress, Movable Type, MetaWeblog and Blogger XML-RPC publishing protocols**) press the **Link** button.

6. To write a post through e-mail, use an e-mail client with the e-mail address you used in Step 1, to create your account. In the **To:** field, enter `post@posterous.com`. The e-mail's **Subject:** line will be your post title. The e-mail message will become the post content. If you want to include pictures into your post, simply attach them to your e-mail and they will be automatically embedded into your post. To publish your post, simply send your e-mail.

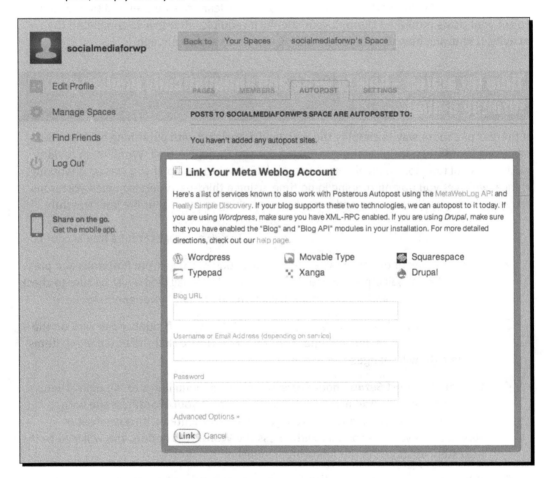

 If you're using a Gmail or Yahoo! account, you'll easily be able to publish posts on-the-go, as most smart phones ship with their respective apps. Note that you cannot edit posts through e-mail, once they've been sent; you'll have to use WordPress instead.

What just happened?

In this brief activity, you first signed up for a free account at Posterous. Then, you configured it to enable the service to write to your WordPress site. Finally, you learned how to publish a post through e-mail.

Posting through Posterous

If you're juggling multiple authors who haven't been acclimated to the publishing process through WordPress, this is a great way to get them writing posts. Sometimes, your writers will want to use Microsoft Word as a means to publishing posts, but they'll usually forget to strip the formatting before pasting the content into WordPress, resulting in different fonts, sizes, and other quirks. Moreover, if they are doing this, they're unnecessarily doubling their workload too. By allowing your content producers to use e-mail as a means of publishing content, there is virtually no learning curve on how to put something online, it's something your site authors have done plenty of times.

As noted earlier, WordPress does provide native functionality to post through e-mail. This process is counter-intuitive, as you need to know your mail server (and whether it's encrypted), port number, deal with some iframe code snippet, or a custom PHP function. In the time it takes you to figure this out, you'll have already published your first post, probably through a cell phone. Posterous, on the other hand, has simplified and polished the entire process, with the help of its 15 million monthly users, making it a seamless effort to publish through e-mail.

Have a go hero

WordPress is malleable. Out of the box, it's a fairly straightforward publishing platform. Over time, as you grow your site, you will undoubtedly encounter some downtime. Remember not to panic. But now that you're fully aware of this fact, how will you prepare? Will you be the next fail whale sensation? You have to stay creative both in terms of engaging your users as well as solving problems. If the majority of your content producers don't feel comfortable using WordPress as a means to publish, can you see yourself running a WordPress site through e-mail groups using Posterous? Everything is a fair question, but you have to ask yourself—*what is the best way to manage your site, before you commit to anything?*

Summary

Managing a large site can seem overwhelming, but with the proper tools and processes in place, you can sleep sound at night, knowing that you've fool-proofed your site, even if it goes down. Here's a rundown of what you've learned:

◆ Hardware, software, and site users are key aspects of maintenance

◆ Creating daily backups using Dropbox can be accomplished in less than seven steps

◆ Your site will go down, even if you go unnoticed. For the time(s) that it becomes unavailable to your users, be sure to make it up to them with special offers or entertain them to lighten the mood.

◆ The WordPress repository houses a handful of useful plugins to make your day-to-day operations a bit easier to manage.

◆ If you're in charge of several content producers, you can let them post through e-mail to keep things simple and user-friendly.

Since content is unique to everyone for any site, we'll go over some social media basics in the last chapter to help you form your voice. We'll also cover some examples on effective strategies, as we go beyond the plugins.

7
Beyond the Plugins Towards True Engagement

*Social media didn't start out through a bunch of WordPress plugins—the Facebook **Share** buttons, the **Tweet This** buttons and the like so it doesn't end with them. It extends well beyond the functionality factor and beyond your WordPress site. Creating buzz and making your social media efforts go viral depends on your content. No book will create that buzz-worthy content for you and, if it were that easy, everything would take off. That's not to say, successful social media implementations are solely reserved for industry experts. It simply means that you need to commit either long-term or short-term and remain proactive.*

Leading up to this chapter, you've learned how to add site features that encourage social connections, automate time-consuming and mundane tasks, measure your campaigns and manage your site. In this final chapter, you'll learn a few tips and tools that delve outside of WordPress. Here's what you'll learn throughout the next several pages:

◆ Engaging visitors comprises of five actions—acknowledging, reciprocating, personalizing, promoting, and repeating.

◆ You'll also learn the importance of instant feedback when it comes to your users.

◆ As Twitter is one of the several mainstays among social media services, you'll follow an activity that teaches you how automatically post a week worth of tweets, using Google Alerts, Bitly, and Yahoo! Pipes.

◆ A frequently downgraded yet important aspect of your site is design, so you'll learn about typography and mobile design.

- In the second activity of this chapter, you'll create a QR code for your print collateral, so you can improve the accessibility of the relationships that you've built online in the real world. You'll also get a breakdown of some do's and don'ts of QR code implementation.

- Last, you'll get more insights as to what social media means beyond the site functionalities, social media networking accounts, and the web.

Let the journey begin.

Engaging site visitors

As a site manager, it's easy to sit back and let your users interact with each other, but you cannot solely rely on them to grow your traffic. Nurturing those social connections within your site can be thought of in these simple steps:

- Acknowledge
- Reciprocate
- Personalize
- Promote
- Repeat

When it comes to social media, staying proactive means you're using certain communication tools and techniques as a gateway to cultivate a genuine discussion, not as a means to cross-promote any products or services. Make no mistake about it, when it comes to using a long-term strategy, your business should come second. That's because once your site users have built deep and solid relationships with each other, they will want to tell their friends about your site. It's equivalent to promoting a great product, which is backed by great customer service. There's a multiplying factor involved. Word of mouth only travels when those words are worth the journey. Nobody wants to promote anything that's half-baked or lacks integrity.

Acknowledge

People have a deep-seeded desire for validation. It goes without saying, but when someone leaves a pingback or comments on your site, tweets to your post, or mentions you in a status update, you have to acknowledge that person. Acknowledgement is not a social media etiquette; it's an Internet etiquette, if you're running a business. Be prompt about it. Facebook, Twitter, MailChimp, Gravity Forms, WordPress, and other services have the capability to provide you with instant push notifications, which can alert you of new messages through e-mail or SMS. There should be no reason for you not to acknowledge people who provide you with feedback on your site. If you're an ardent Twitter user, take advantage of the `#FollowFriday` (`#ff`) hashtag to call out the people who like your site. It won't take you a lot of time to reply with a quick thank you, and it'll keep your visitors happy.

Reciprocate

Reciprocating is not a synonym for acknowledging. It means to give back. There's no requisite for giving back either. When you want to build a following on your site or any other social network, you'll want to provide your users with relevant content music, pictures, white papers, downloads, videos, or anything else that matters to them. That content does not have to come from you; you can be a portal site for your niche, if there's a demand for it. Content can come from anywhere, as long as it relates to your site visitors.

While it may work for TV adverts, oftentimes, the more you push your products or services through Facebook updates or tweets, the less likely they'll want to follow you. The web is more direct and personal. Spewing a bunch of promotional messages, in hopes you'll capture a small percentage of prospective site users is not a good tactic. Whatever your web endeavours are, the likelihood is palpable that there are a significant number of competitors within your field of interest. Moreover, most content is freely available online, making the incentive to stay on your site tougher.

You have the tools to gauge your visitors' interests, be it through Google Analytics, YouTube Analytics, Facebook Insights, and so on. Knowing how they're entering your site and how much time they spend on a certain page, you can use that to your advantage in giving them what they want. In turn, you can make that a starting point for your social media campaigns.

Personalize

Automation is not a bad thing, especially when it comes to saving you time to focus on important aspects of your site. However, don't rely on automating processes that are intended to be performed by you, a real human being. Twitter is notorious for allowing users to send out automated Direct Messages to people who've been automatically followed. This is as effective as sending out a canned message to your parents when you thank them for your birthday present. It's not genuine. A Direct Message has the intention of being personal, so save a few minutes throughout the day to properly send out tailored messages.

By the way how web has matured throughout the last few years, we've been accustomed to anonymity, remaining ambiguous and, generally, being desensitized to anything that pops up on our screens. Social media and social engagement aim to bring back that human touch. If you're the type of person that finds it uneasy to chitchat at an office party or networking event, you'll most likely experience some of the same challenges online. It doesn't mean that you'll be awful at building a good rapport and making your site intriguing to others, but you'll need to give it a few tries to become a natural at it.

Promote

If you've ever been in charge of a blog, you'll have first-hand experience of feeling the pressure to publish a post when you've depleted all the desire to write it. When it comes to social media content, however, the rules are a bit different. You don't always have to publish original content, as previously mentioned. The content can come from a random user on your BuddyPress network, forum, or a VIP member. It can also come from an entirely different site through one of your Yahoo! Pipes. But what's key to your content is promotion, which is a bit tricky in itself. If you don't promote content, your traffic will stagnate. If you promote too many things too many times, you'll lose people's interest. Finding the perfect balance will take some testing, but if you keep up with your analytics on a regular basis, you'll narrow it down.

If you know influential people in your industry, reach out to them and see if they're willing to help you promote your products or services. Typically, they'll work with you as long as you ask politely and reciprocate the favour. You'll also want to go outside of the web to sprout some word of mouth, doing it the old fashioned way and taking these avenues:

- **Attend industry events and network**: Be ready to give your 10-second elevator pitch about your site and have several business cards on you to hand out.

- **Go local and put up flyers for your site**: Book stores, apartment complexes, college campuses, and coffee houses usually have a dedicated pinup wall where you can promote your products and services without much hassle.

- **Use traditional media gateways**: Wherever you live, there's a good chance that there's a local TV or radio program you can pitch to. There is, perhaps, an even greater chance you can score an interview with a local magazine or newspaper. Again, be prepared to give your 10-second elevator pitch about your site, but don't aim for prime time unless you're absolutely ready.

- **Tell your family and friends**: It may seem like you're asking them for a favour, but you probably won't get a bigger stamp of approval than from the people who know you best. If it's something they're hesitant to do, don't be afraid to ask why. They may provide you with some valuable feedback than can help you.

Repeat

Repetition is where most social media efforts fall off the bandwagon. It can be discouraging, at times, to produce, promote, and expect amazing content to rise to the top only to see it plateau, when it results in a lack of social engagement. It's during these critical times that you might experience a tendency to dedicate less time and effort on your strategies. But before you excuse social media as a whole, try these tips instead:

- **Repost**: Online media is unlike traditional print media, which has to go through several time-consuming and costly phases. If you have content that didn't get the appropriate attention it deserved, repost it again. It's quick, easy, and free.

◆ **Follow up**: Produce or find related content and link it to your existing content to pique your users' interest. Sometimes, the most intriguing things people learn online are by stumbling upon them; you just have to ensure that serendipity is capable of happening.

◆ **Syndicate**: Approach other people in your industry and ask them if they'd be interested in publishing your content through their networks. They might ask you to edit a few things to make it fit their user base, but it's a small effort worth the exchange.

Likewise, once you've honed down your social media skills, don't get too lax with your daily tasks. Unless you have a short-term social media strategy, you're in it for the long haul, which means you need to stay persistent in producing and promoting your content. Establish a frequency that works with your schedule and adhere to it.

Time for action – how to automatically tweet custom content

In this three-part activity, we'll fetch some custom content through Google Alerts, then port it over to **Yahoo! Pipes** and publish all the scheduled tweets using **WordPress**. You will need a Google and Twitter account, as well. Let's get started:

Part 1—Creating custom Google Alerts

1. Log on to http://www.google.com/alerts, using your free Google account. If you haven't created one yet, log on to https://accounts.google.com/NewAccount.

2. To create your first Google Alert, enter a keyword that would apply to your Twitter followers in the **Search query** field. For our example, we'll enter social media.

3. To retrieve all relevant social media content, select **Everything** from the **Result type** drop-down selection. Select **Once a day** for **How often**, and select **Only the best results** for **How many**, as shown in the following screenshot:

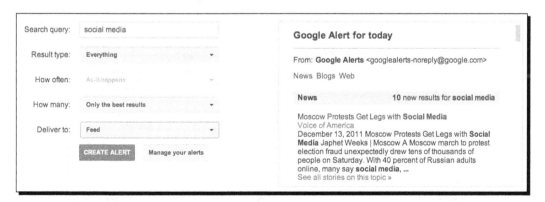

4. Select **Feed** for the **Deliver to** drop-down selection, and press the **CREATE ALERT** button to create your first Google Alert RSS feed, as shown in the screenshot.

5. Repeat Steps 2 to 4 for another Google Alert that also focuses on your particular niche. For example, we'll enter `wordpress`.

6. On the next screen, click on the orange RSS icon next to the **Google Reader** link under the **Deliver** column label for each alert, as shown in the following screenshot. This will bring up your social media RSS feed. Copy both web addresses into your clipboard or note application for the next part:

Part 2—Automatically formatting your content for Twitter

1. Log on to `http://bitly.com/` and register with a free account and sign in, if you're not using your Twitter or Facebook credentials. Once signed in, click on your username to reveal the drop-down menu and click on **Settings**. Then, copy the **API Key** into a text editor:

2. Now, log on to `http://pipes.yahoo.com` and sign up for a free account, if you don't have a Facebook or Google account.

3. Next, visit `http://pipes.yahoo.com/socialmediaforwp/feedblender` and click on the **Clone** button under the **Pipe** title. Notice that the **Pipe** title changes ending in **copy** on the next screen. You can edit it by clicking on the title itself, as shown in the following screenshot:

4. Press the **Edit Source** button located under the **Pipe** Web Address to access the pipe view and modify it to tailor to your content.

5. Replace the Google Alert RSS Feeds in the **Fetch Feed** module with your own from *Part 1*.

6. The **Regex** module is responsible for stripping any unexpected HTML code that may be present in the feed titles as well as hash tagging keywords within the feed titles, as show in the following screenshot. Be sure to modify the existing filters within the **Regex** module to accommodate your own content. For example, if your content tailors toward soccer, you may want to create a new **Rule** that replaces soccer with #soccer in the existing rules:

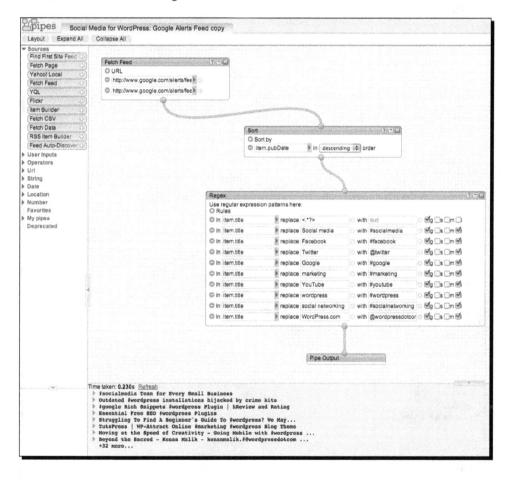

7. Once you're satisfied with the **Output** results, save your pipe and click on the **Back to My Pipes** link located near the **Save** button in the upper-right corner, which will bring you to a page listing all your Yahoo! Pipes.

8. Click on the pipe you just saved and press the **Publish** button on the following screen. Then, click on the **Get as RSS** link and copy the URL from the following screen, which is the RSS feed output for your pipe.

9. Log on to `http://pipes.yahoo.com/socialmediaforwp/autotweet` and customize the pipe by repeating the processes described in Step 2 and 3. Replace the feed from the **Fetch Feed** module with your own feed from Step 7.

10. Connect Yahoo! Pipes to bitly by editing the first **Loop** module that's connected to the **Fetch Feed** module. Do this by replacing the current bitly login name which is `socialmediaforwp`, with your own username for the login field, as shown in the following screenshot. Then, replace the **apiKey** value with your own API key from Step 1:

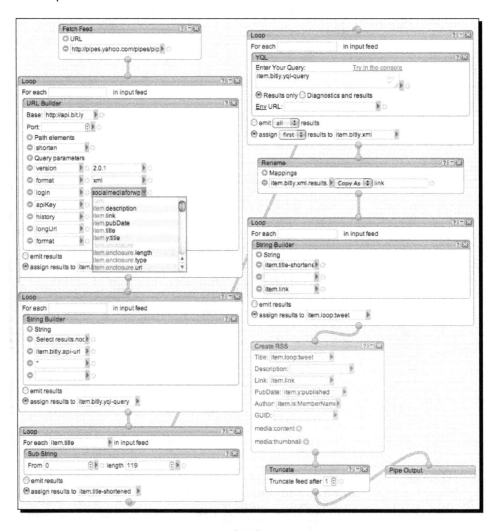

11. If you select and highlight the **Output** module, you should now see one feed item for your hashtagged content from Google Alerts in the **debugger** pane. You can throttle the amount of RSS feed results (that is, tweets) by changing the numerical value in the **Truncate** module that's connected to the **Output** module. Once you're satisfied, save your changes and copy the pipe RSS feed URL by repeating Steps 7 and 8.

Part 3—Automatically tweeting your content

 Steps 1 through 7 of this activity are identical to Part 2 of *How to automatically display selective forum posts in Twitter* in *Chapter 5, Keeping Up with the Stats*. For more visual guidance, please refer to that chapter.

1. In your WordPress site, navigate to **Add New** under **Plugins** and search for a **WP to Twitter** plugin. Install and active the plugin.

2. Navigate to **WP to Twitter** under **Settings** and follow the steps to connect Twitter to your WordPress site by first logging on to Twitter's application registration page at `https://dev.twitter.com/apps/new`. Give your application an appropriate name and description, and use the URL for your site in the **WebSite** field. The **Callback URL** is not required, so we'll skip that for now, as you can always edit it later.

3. Accept the terms and conditions, and press the **Create your Twitter application** button.

4. Once your Twitter application has been created, navigate to the **Settings** tab near the top and select **Read and Write** for the **Access level** under **Application Type**. This will allow WordPress to post information to Twitter. Be sure to press the **Update this Twitter application's settings** button near the bottom of the page to save your changes.

5. Next, press the **Details** tab near the top and press the **Create my access token** button in the **Your access token** section near the bottom. This will create the **Access Token** as well as the **Access Token Secret**. Make sure that the **Access level** shows **Read and Write**. If it does not, go back to Step 5 and make sure **Read and Write** is selected and create a new token with the updated settings.

6. Back in WordPress, fill in all the appropriate information to connect Twitter with your site and press the **Connect to Twitter** button in **WP to Twitter** under **Settings**.

7. Once connected, make sure to uncheck **Update when a post is edited** under **Basic Settings**, as you don't want to tweet old content. Keep all other default values. Also, select **Use bitly as a URL shortener** from the **Choose your short URL service** drop-down selection, as you don't want to display long URLs in your tweets. Press the **Save WP | Twitter options** button to save your changes.

8. Navigate to **Categories** under **Posts** and create a new category named **autotweet**.

9. Last, navigate back to **WP to Twitter** under **Settings** and select **autotweet** from the **Limit Updating Categories** section at the bottom, so that only content stored in that category will be tweeted, as shown in the following screenshot. Press the **Set Categories** button to save your changes:

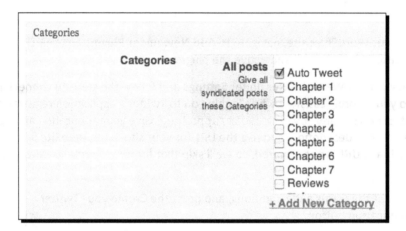

10. Next, we'll add another plugin by navigating to **Add New** under **Plugins** and searching for a plugin labelled **FeedWordPress**. Install and activate the plugin.

11. Navigate to **Syndication** under **Syndication**, and paste the RSS feed address from Step 11 of *Part 2* in the text field labelled **New source: Website or feed URI**, then press the **Add button** and press the **Use this feed** button on the following screen.

12. Once you've returned to the main **Syndication** settings page, hover over the feed title you added in the previous step and press the **Categories** link. Scroll down to the **Categories** section and check the **autotweet** category you created in Step 8, as shown in the screenshot. Finally, be sure to press the **Save Changes** button to save your settings.

What just happened?

In the first part, we learned how to set up Google Alerts on a topic that might be interesting for our site users. We saved the alert as an RSS feed, so we could import the content into Yahoo! Pipes for the next part. Yahoo! Pipes allowed us to customize the Google Alert post titles, which were being used as tweets. The service also allowed us to automatically convert certain keywords into hashtags. After we completed our edits in Yahoo! Pipes, we exported the Twitter content as an RSS feed, so we could import it into WordPress in the last part. Using a couple of WordPress plugins, we were able to automatically post tweets several times a day, so we could spend less time providing relevant content to entice our users and spend more time developing our social connections.

Google Alerts and Yahoo! Pipes

Chapter 1, and Chapter 3 made extensive usage of Yahoo! Pipes, so to continue on the trend of maximizing this free online resource, we learned more about utilizing the different pipe operators used to automate the hashtagging process. While it's possible to aggregate content based on certain keywords, using Pipes, Google Alert's main advantage is the simplicity of setting up. As the majority of Internet users still rely on Google as a search engine with its non-stop fine-tuning, it makes perfect sense to cut down on all the guess work it would take to replicate the search results for your keywords or hashtags using Pipes. As a result, all you have to do is enter your query, do some cut-and-pasting of information for Pipes, bitly and WordPress, and, voila, you're all set!

Using automated tweets to supplement original tweets

Once you've finished the activity outlined in this chapter, your site is set to tweet automatically anywhere between two to five times per day, if the Google Alert keywords are popular enough to produce a constant stream of search results. The amounts of tweets per day can be easily adjusted using the **Truncate** module, as mentioned earlier. While you'll save a lot of time maintaining your Twitter account with relevant content, keep in mind, however, that these tweets should not be used in place of writing your own but rather to supplement your existing ones.

Pop quiz – social media artillery

1. Most services discussed throughout this book allow push notifications to alert you of new updates.

    a. True

    b. False

2. Five essential actions to follow for successful social media strategies include acknowledgement, reciprocation, personalization, promotion and repetition.

   a. True

   b. False

3. Yahoo! Pipes allows you to automatically hashtag your content.

   a. True

   b. False

4. Once you've gotten your Twitter account on auto-pilot, you'll start receiving many more followers.

   a. True

   b. False

5. You cannot use Yahoo! Pipes in conjuction with Google Alerts and WordPress.

   a. True

   b. False

Design speaks

A lot of site managers tend to believe design should not be a top priority, because a sleek site without any good content is just a site with some pretty decorations. While there is a lot of truth to this opinion, there are two sides, of course. A site with good content that's terribly designed does not only lack vision, but it usually lacks user experience, authority, and credibility. Design is how you present yourself. It can break down into dozens of tiny aspects, but we'll just focus on some of the broader elements that pertain to your site and social media.

The essence of typography

If design is how you dress yourself, then typography is what type of shoes you wear. Footwear not only affects posture and stride, but it also suggests personality and lifestyle; typography is no different. Your mental image of someone wearing sandals probably differs from someone wearing cowboy boots. In this same regard, typography suggests tone and discipline. The typeface, leading, kerning and all other attributes influence how you communicate with others online or in print. Are your fonts big, bold, and loud or are they demure, curly, and bespoke?

A few years ago, it was considered a valiant attempt to use fonts other than *Arial* or *Times Roman* on websites. Custom font implementations such as, *sIFR*, *cufón* and *FLIR* were inundated with precautionary notices, which typically addressed certain usage limits and browser incompatibilities. Only recently through services such as Google Fonts, TypeKit, Fontspring, and Font Squirrel have sites been able to easily utilize custom web fonts. If you haven't taken advantage of them, do so now! Don't limit the way you present yourself with a run-of-the-mill font. Choose fonts that speak to you and your users, and they'll appreciate the attention to detail, if only subconsciously.

Mobile design—ushering in a new standard

There is a good reason why Facebook is devoting a lot of their resources to mobile application development. Not everybody owns a new computer, but most people carry smartphones. Cellphone manufacturers have ushered in the next wave of online relationships with the rise of affordable smartphones, tablets, and Google's open source Android platform. Yet with the swift advances in mobile technology, a lot of websites still lack accessibility.

Responsive and adaptive web development was just as popular, or unpopular, a few years ago as using custom web fonts. It was an arduous process trying to avoid pinch-zooming on mobile devices with custom scripts that would work cross-platform, cross-browser across multiple browser versions. With Microsoft's Internet Explorer development team now taking a proactive approach in following suit with media queries, CSS3, and web standards, it's imperative you do the same. It's where everyone is headed. The sooner you can accommodate the people who are already equipped with the hardware and software to build connections through their preferred method of communication, the better off you are at making your social media efforts more effective. Need more convincing? Just peruse the following statistics:

- As of 2011, the mobile market consists of four billion mobile phones in use with 1.08 billions consisting of smartphones.
- By 2014, the projected amount of mobile Internet users should take over desktop Internet users.
- Half of all local searches are performed on a mobile device.
- Some 86 percent of mobile Internet users are using their devices while watching TV. Americans, on average, spend 2.7 hours per day socializing on them and 91 percent of mobile Internet access is to socialize.
- More than 33 percent of Facebook's 600 million-plus user base uses Facebook Mobile; Twitter has 165 million users of whom half of them use the Twitter Mobile application.

Don't let these numbers scare you. If you don't have the resources to hire mobile application developers or web designers who can transform your WordPress site into a mobile-friendly one, accommodating this growing group of mobile users can be as easy as searching the WordPress repository for responsive themes. Just start with the basics and upgrade whenever you can.

Beyond the Web

Switching mediums doesn't dictate what you can and cannot do. A couple of years ago, print posters that promoted events, products, or services often displayed a web address, which would often result in people following these steps:

- Launching a browser application on the mobile device
- Click into the address bar
- Try to type in a long web address that consisted of many special characters while also walking around
- Retype the long web address because of some typo as a result of walking around
- Load the page again

It was a frustrating process until Quick Response (QR) codes became popular. Unlike traditional barcodes, which are capable of only displaying data like product prices or descriptions, QR codes are capable of much more like browsing or bookmarking a website. All a user has to do is scan the code, leaving the rest up to the smartphone or tablet. It's just another way to make your relationship with your users more accessible. Following is a list of more advanced usages of QR codes:

- Promote your business, service, or event on a map through Google's or Bing's maps
- Receive additional information online, if there's limited space on the print collateral
- Get special discount codes or coupons
- Streamline the offline experience with the online experience
- Gathering feedback for polls and opinions

In the activity ahead, you'll create your very own QR code to make it easier for your users to engage with you by redirecting them to your site.

Time for action – how to create a vector-based QR code for print production

You don't need a degree in design or expensive software to produce a fancy-looking QR code that will point your visitors to your site. All you really need is about five minutes and a link. Here's how you do it:

1. Log on to `http://keremerkan.net/qr-code-and-2d-code-generator/`.

2. Select the **Browse to a Website** for the **Select a Code Action** drop-down selection.

3. Enter the web address you want to promote in the **Web Site URL** text field.

4. Select **None** for the **URL Shortening** drop-down selection; select **Low** for the **Error Correction Level** drop-down selection; select **10** for the **Block Size in Pixels** drop-down selection; select **1** for the **Margin Size in Blocks** drop-down selection, and select **Encapsulated Postscript (EPS)** for the **Output Type** drop-down selection, as shown in the screenshot:

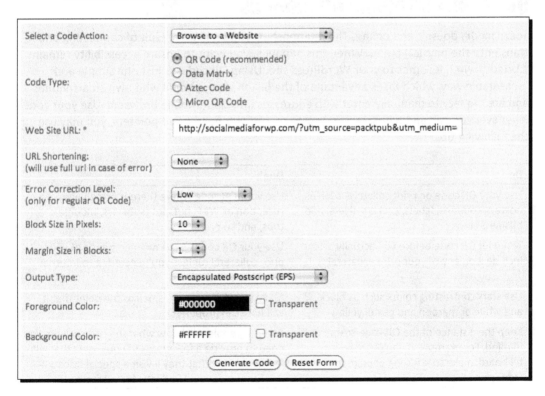

5. If you want to match the QR code with the branding of your print collateral, you can choose a different foreground and background color other than black and white. However, be sure to have a strong contrast between the two colors, so your QR code will scan correctly.

6. Press the **Generate Code** button, which will save the `.eps` file to your computer.

This online QR code generator is capable of using any link, so take advantage of this feature by tracking your link, using Google's URL Builder, as described in Chapter 5, *Keeping Up with the Stats*.

What just happened?

In this quick activity, we created a QR code, which launched a link on the device that's being used to scan the code. The QR code was then produced and saved as a vector file, so we could use it on our print collateral.

QR codes and online promotions

Social media doesn't end online. The relationships you build as a result of connecting online transfer to the physical realm. When this happens, you want to ensure accessibility remains a priority when it comes to your WordPress site. Using QR codes is just one simple and measurable way, which takes advantage of the billion savvy people who own smartphones and are too lazy to manually enter web addresses into their mobile browsers. Use your code whenever you can and wherever it's appropriate. If you need more pointers, you may use the following tips:

Do	Don't
Use your QR code on print collateral such as posters, coupons, labels, stickers, flyers, and business cards	Use your QR code where there is no cell phone reception or Wi-Fi hotspot (subways, mountain tops, and so on)
Test your QR code before you actually include it on any of your print collateral	Use your QR code as the main emphasis of your print collateral (unless you're catering to Internet devotees and the like)
Use stark contrasting colors such as black and white or maroon and pastel yellow	Make your QR code too small to the point that it will not scan properly
Keep the distance of the QR code scanning in mind. For example, if you put it on a billboard, make sure it's big enough to scan from afar.	Assume people will know what the code will do. You need to provide a few words to your users that will let them know that they'll visit a special discount link for one of your products, for example.

For a more visual take on how you should not implement QR codes, visit `http://wtfqrcodes.com`.

QR Codes and Microsoft tag

QR codes are one of the most popular barcodes to date that provide a rich feature set to allow you to extend your online reach to the real world. They've been around for several years and they have been adopted in ads by many major brands such as Coca Cola, Ford, and Starbucks. However, they're not the only major player in the space of barcodes. Microsoft has its own version called Tag, which is a bit more design-friendly than QR codes. The Tag barcode is even promoted through its own website (`http://tag.microsoft.com`), which lets you not only save in multiple formats but also allows you to save QR codes for free, as well. It does not, however, support saving in EPS format.

The right format for the right job

Not many sites exist online, which allow you to generate QR codes in EPS format. Generally, it's not a big deal, unless you've hired a print designer to produce all your materials. If you give your designer a JPG or PNG version of your QR code, prepare to hear a few loud belly laughs, as those formats are not conducive for high-resolution print collateral. The EPS format is lossless in quality, in comparison, as it can be infinitely scaled up while still retaining every detail. The disadvantage to using an EPS file, of course, is that you'll need a program that can import it. Adobe Illustrator, Fireworks, Photoshop, or the popular free software GIMP.

Have a go hero

Social media goes well beyond your website, Facebook group, and Twitter account. People may discover you through a flyer that was posted at a college campus or bar. Using what you've learned in this book, you can produce some eye-catching creative, include a traceable QR code to your Twitter account, and use Yahoo! Pipes and WordPress to build more relationships. All of these tools are appendages for your online presence, but you still control how to reach out to people and connect each other. From VIP memberships to forums and BuddyPress installations, you have all the tools you need to make your WordPress site more interactive. As they say, the sky is the limit.

Summary

Social Media are two ominous buzzwords that don't mean much, unless what you do is social in nature and the media, or content, you provide is relevant to your users. Billions of Internet users own billions of phones and produce billions of tweets. Attempting to earn the attention of just a small slice of those online users on a global level is no easier feat than trying to do the same in the real world on a local level. Sure, there are plugins, snippets and add-ons, which can assist you in getting more engagement out of your WordPress users, but everything falls back to content. Your users need to be able to react to it, which means you need to supply accessible, relevant, and useful, if not entertaining, content. This last chapter provided you with the last few titbits of advice. Here's the rundown of what you just learned:

◆ You need to facilitate the following:

  ❑ acknowledgement

  ❑ reciprocation

  ❑ personalization

  ❑ promotion

  ❑ repetition

◆ If some of your content is worth repeating, repeat it—rehash, repost, and republish.

◆ Typography can have a huge impact on how you present yourself online and has become easily accessible through Google Fonts and other web font services.

◆ If you haven't thought about responsive web design, start now, because the mobile market consists of 1.08 billion smartphones and will eventually take over the desktop market.

◆ QR codes are an effective means to take online social media promotions and transfer them to the real world.

For the average WordPress user, this book attempts to provide concepts to create a more interactive site and stimulate social engagement. The activities can often be mixed and mashed with each other, leaving ample room for you to discover your most effective way in forming connections and building stronger relationships. Every site owner has its own unique voice, resources, and preferences, making the social media strategy a commitment that is also unique in itself. Just remember—be passionate, put out good content, and make it pretty.

Further Reading

This book makes ample use of researched facts and statistics to provide context. As social media is partly about sharing, this appendix provides all the relevant attribution as well as other helpful articles, in the event you want to reference the information for any of your own projects. Supplementary material such as downloads and other material can be accessed at `http://SocialMediaforWP.com`.

Chapter 1—Share it the Easy Way

- Wael Ghonim—Creating a 'Revolution 2.0' in Egypt `http://www.npr.org/2012/02/09/146636605/wael-ghonim-creating-a-revolution-2-0-in-egypt`

- As Obama does the Twitter `http://mashable.com/2007/04/27/obama-twitter/`

- Barack Obama's MySpace ambitions `http://mashable.com/2007/02/11/barack-obama/`

- How Obama's Internet campaign changed politics `http://bits.blogs.nytimes.com/2008/11/07/how-obamas-internet-campaign-changed-politics/`

- Salman Khan—Let's use video to reinvent education `http://www.ted.com/talks/salman_khan_let_s_use_video_to_reinvent_education.html`

- Japan Earthquake and Tsunami—Social Media Spreads News, Raises Relief Funds `http://abcnews.go.com/Technology/japan-earthquake-tsunami-drive-social-media-dialogue/story?id=13117677#.Tu0CUyPLwng`

- Millennium bug hits retailers `http://news.bbc.co.uk/2/hi/business/582007.stm`

- Minor bug problems arise `http://news.bbc.co.uk/2/hi/science/nature/586620.stm`

- Y2K travel warning issued `http://www.abc.net.au/am/stories/s69974.htm`

- Web Squared—Web 2.0 five years on `http://www.web2summit.com/web2009/public/schedule/detail/10194`

- Mainstream media usage of Web 2.0 Services is increasing `http://www.readwriteweb.com/archives/mainstream_media_web20.php`

- Riding the waves of "Web 2.0" `http://www.pewinternet.org/Reports/2006/Riding-the-Waves-of-Web-20/Riding-the-Waves.aspx`

Chapter 2—Building the Social Network: BuddyPress and WP Symposium

- Timeline of Facebook `http://en.wikipedia.org/wiki/Timeline_of_Facebook`

- At last—The full story of how Facebook was founded `http://www.businessinsider.com/how-facebook-was-founded-2010-3`

- Facebook's Mark Zuckerberg—hacker, dropout, CEO `http://www.fastcompany.com/magazine/115/open_features-hacker-dropout-ceo.html?page=0%2C1`

- BP Privacy—History and lessons learned from developing a Major BuddyPress component `http://jeffsayre.com/2011/01/19/bp-privacy-history-and-lessons-learned-from-developing-a-major-buddypress-component/`

- Gamification—How competition is reinventing business, marketing, and everyday life `http://mashable.com/2011/07/28/gamification/`

Chapter 3—Community Forums for the Masses

- Forum software timeline 1994 - 2011 `http://www.forum-software.org/forum-software-timeline-from-1994-to-today`

- How to survive a tech support call `http://www.nytimes.com/2006/02/22/technology/circuits/23POGUE-EMAIL.html`
- Inside Zappos—A culture of customer service `http://advisor.inc.com/inside-zappos-a-culture-of-customer-service`
- One hundred million voices `http://blog.twitter.com/2011/09/one-hundred-million-voices.html`

Chapter 4—VIP Memberships

- The new rules of building customer loyalty `http://www.inc.com/guides/201105/new-rules-of-building-customer-loyalty.html`
- The difference between a bonus and free `http://sethgodin.typepad.com/seths_blog/2010/01/the-difference-between-a-bonus-and-free.html`
- How to combine foursquare and your loyalty program `http://www.inc.com/guides/201107/how-to-combine-foursquare-and-your-loyalty-program.html`
- When will educators get serious about gaming? `http://blogs.hbr.org/innovations-in-education/2011/03/when-will-educators-get-seriou.html`
- How to start a customer rewards program `http://www.inc.com/guides/2010/08/how-to-start-a-customer-rewards-program.html`
- Serious play—The business of social currency `http://blogs.hbr.org/cs/2011/04/serious_play_the_business_of_s.html`

Chapter 5—Keeping Up with the Stats

- Internet 2010 in numbers `http://royal.pingdom.com/2011/01/12/internet-2010-in-numbers/`
- What's the difference between clicks, visits, visitors, pageviews, and unique pageviews? `https://support.google.com/googleanalytics/bin/answer.py?hl=en&answer=57164`
- What's the difference between the Absolute Unique Visitor report and the New versus. Returning' report? `http://support.google.com/googleanalytics/bin/answer.py?hl=en-GB&answer=113734`
- What does bounce rate mean? `http://support.google.com/googleanalytics/bin/answer.py?hl=en&answer=81986`

◆ Understanding campaign variables—The five dimensions of campaign tracking `http://support.google.com/googleanalytics/bin/answer.py?hl=en&answer=55579`

Chapter 6—Managing your Site

◆ Unauthorized access hits Sony PlayStation accounts `http://news.yahoo.com/unauthorized-access-hits-sony-playstation-accounts-032717845.html`

◆ BlackBerry outage for three days caused by faulty router says former RIM staffer `http://www.guardian.co.uk/technology/2011/oct/14/blackberry-outage-faulty-router-suspected`

◆ BlackBerrys buzz back to life after a long outage `http://on.msnbc.com/vmCE43`

◆ WordPress.com suffers Largest DDoS attack in its history `http://techcrunch.com/2011/03/03/wordpress-com-suffers-major-ddos-attack/`

◆ WordPress hit with massive hack attack `http://www.huffingtonpost.com/2011/03/03/wordpress-down-ddos-attack_n_830958.html`

◆ The Zappos Way of managing `http://www.inc.com/magazine/20090501/the-zappos-way-of-managing.html`

◆ It's time to fire some of your customers `http://blogs.hbr.org/tjan/2011/08/its-time-to-fire-some-of-your.html`

◆ Before you link pay to customer feedback—five essentials `http://blogs.hbr.org/cs/2011/09/how_to_link_pay_to_customer_fe.html`

◆ Is Facebook Beacon a privacy nightmare? `http://gigaom.com/2007/11/06/facebook-beacon-privacy-issues/`

◆ RIP Facebook Beacon `http://mashable.com/2009/09/19/facebook-beacon-rip/`

◆ Dropbox case study—epic scale, one year later `http://www.justin.tv/startuplessonslearned/b/286528406`

◆ Managing your reputation in a world of crowd sourcing `http://blogs.hbr.org/cs/2008/03/managing_your_reputation_in_a.html`

◆ Why you might choose to be in favor of transparency `http://sethgodin.typepad.com/seths_blog/2011/04/why-you-might-be-in-favor-of-transparency.html`

Chapter 7—Beyond the Plugins Towards True Engagement

- The size of the mobile market `http://cache.gawkerassets.com/assets/images/4/2010/03/090903-is-mobile.png`

- Mary Meeker—mobile internet will soon overtake fixed Internet `http://gigaom.com/2010/04/12/mary-meeker-mobile-internet-will-soon-overtake-fixed-internet/`.

- comScore releases inaugural report, *The 2010 Mobile Year in Review* `http://www.comscore.com/Press_Events/Press_Releases/2011/2/comScore_Releases_Inaugural_Report_The_2010_Mobile_Year_in_Review`

- The mobile Internet report `http://www.morganstanley.com/institutional/techresearch/pdfs/mobile_internet_report.pdf`.

- The United State of Social and Mobile Marketing `http://searchengineland.com/the-united-state-of-social-mobile-marketing-63511`.

- Facebook CTO—Mobile is 2011 priority `http://blogs.wsj.com/digits/2011/01/25/facebook-cto-mobile-is-2011-priority/`

- Coca-Cola launches its first U.S QR code program `http://news.yahoo.com/coca-cola-launches-first-u-qr-code-program-171016607.html`

- Facebook statistics `http://www.facebook.com/press/info.php?statistics`

- The big web show #1: web fonts `http://5by5.tv/bigwebshow/1`

- Starbucks QR codes offer rich BLEND of info `http://mashable.com/2011/10/26/starbucks-qr-codes/`

- QR Code scavenger hunt offers ford Fiesta as prize `http://mashable.com/2010/12/14/qr-code-scavenger-hunt/`

- Data Monday: Consuming News on Mobile Devices `http://www.lukew.com/ff/entry.asp?1461`

- Responsive Web Design `http://www.alistapart.com/articles/responsive-web-design/`

- Mobile First `http://www.lukew.com/presos/preso.asp?26`

- What is Tag? `http://tag.microsoft.com/what-is-tag/home.aspx`

- 10 fascinating Youtube facts that may surprise you `http://mashable.com/2011/02/19/youtube-facts/`

Pop Quiz Answers

Chapter 1, Share it the Easy Way

1.	An ESP allows you to connect RSS feeds together.	Answer: B Yahoo! Pipes allows you to connect RSS feeds together.
2.	You can only use one RSS feed source at a time when building a Yahoo! Pipe.	Answer: B You can use as many RSS feed sources as you like.
3.	Ping-O-Matic allows you to collect subscriber information for mailing campaigns.	Answer: B Ping-O-Matic is a service that notifies your WordPress site and search engines that your blog has updated.
4.	The process in which you collect information from prospective customers on whether they are interested in your content is called lead generation	Answer: A
5.	You can use Yahoo! Pipes to customize any and all of your WordPress RSS feeds?	Answer: A

Chapter 2, Building the Social Network: BuddyPress and WP Symposium

BuddyPress Basics		
1.	You can set up your BP-powered site in five minutes?	Answer: A
2.	The broader you keep your site, the more people you'll attract	Answer: B While on rare occasions you can attract more people to your site by broadening the area of focus on your site; generally, the more niche you go, the better chances you have of running a popular BP-powered site.
3	All WordPress and BuddyPress plugins are free.	Answer: B All WordPress themes and plugins are free on the official WordPress repository, but there are a handful of theme and plugin shops online that charge for premium products and support.
4.	Gamification is the process of adding gaming components to engage your audience?	Answer: A
5.	Integrating a Facebook with WordPress is considered bad practice?	Answer: B With hundreds of million Facebook users already accustomed to using the **Login with Facebook** button, you'll lower the barrier of entry by allowing them to access your site when you integrate FB with WP.
Audience engagement		
1.	You need to use WP-FB Autoconnect to take advantage of the Achievements page?	Answer: B While it's recommended that you use the WP-FB **Autoconnect** plugin on your site for greater reach, it is not a requirement of Achievements for BuddyPress.
2.	Try to reward your visitors with multiple popups, as they need to be engaged	Answer: B The last thing you want to do is bombard site visitors with incessant pop-ups. Use them sparingly for online promotions or special announcements.

3.	Providing as much information as you can fit into your Welcome Page is detrimental to the success of the initial visit for a new site user	Answer: B It's easy to fill up your **Welcome** page with a long list of site features and other information, but try to stick to the basics of why your site matters to your users, what type of information is available and how they can utilize it.
4.	You can use any point system when you create Achievements	Answer: A
5.	Progressive profiling means that you'll learn more information about your site visitors every time they log in	Answer: B Progressive profiling means you'll learn more information about your site visitors every time they complete an action that you can track. For example, using Achievements for BuddyPress, you can get a more accurate representation of your visitor based on the achievement he or she has completed. This can occur on separate site visits as well as during the same site visit.

Chapter 3, Community Forums for the Masses

1.	bbPress requires running BuddyPress on your site	Answer: B The latest release of bbPress does not require BuddyPress to function, but it does require WordPress.
2.	Group forums do not have any privacy settings?	Answer: B bbPress has three visibility options for your forums. They include public, hidden, and private.
3.	FeedWordPress is a content syndication plugin?	Answer: A
4.	Regex stands for regular expression and is capable of matching text?	Answer: A
5.	It's never a good idea to segment content?	Answer: B It's a good idea to segment content to improve your reach. Covering a single broad topic may not cater to the majority of your users. Always provide (customizable) options for content to your users to improve their site experience.

Chapter 4, VIP Memberships

1.	All memberships have to be VIP Memberships.	Answer: B Your memberships can be anything you like, but they have to be worth the time it takes to sign up. If there's no good incentive, you'll have a tough time trying to recruit new members.
2.	CubePoints is an excellent alternative to BuddyPress.	Answer: B CubePoints is an excellent alternative to Achievements for BuddyPress.
3.	S2 Member supports paid memberships.	Answer: A
4.	CVP is an acronym for constant value perimeter.	Answer: B CVP is an acronym for Customer Value Proposition.
5.	BuddyPress integrates with CubePoints and S2 Member.	Answer: A

Chapter 5, Keeping Up with the Stats

1.	Hits are accurate metrics for site traffic	Answer: B Hits are fairly inaccurate metrics for site traffic. Absolute unique visitors are far more accurate.
2.	Bounce rate refers to the percentage of visitors who leave your page upon arriving to it.	Answer: A
3.	Unique pageviews are more accurate than regular pageviews in Google Analytics.	Answer: A
4.	Google's URL Builder is a useful URL shortening service.	Answer: B Google's URL Builder will actually lengthen your URL but, in exchange, you'll be able to measure your marketing campaign within Google Analytics.
5.	It takes 24 hours for a full, accurate set of data to appear in Google Analytics.	Answer: A

Chapter 6, Managing your Site

| 1. | Three key aspects to WordPress maintenance are Beacon, BuddyPress and Boxdrop. | Answer: B

When it comes to site management, three key aspects of any site include hardware, software, and site users. |
|---|---|---|
| 2. | A site user is a blanket term for a visitor, member, administrator, and anybody else that accesses or uses your site. | Answer: A |
| 3. | You should back up your site on a daily basis. | Answer: A |
| 4. | You can experience more than 40 minutes of downtime with 99.9 percent server availability. | Answer: A |
| 5. | You should set your permission bits to 644 when creating your backup folder. | Answer: B

Unless you have a custom-rigged backup solution for your WordPress site, generally, your permission bits need to be set to 755. This means the owner of the file has permission to read, write, and execute; the group and everyone else has permission to only read and execute. |

Chapter 7, Beyond the Plugins Towards True Engagement

1.	Most services discussed throughout this book allow push notifications to alert you of new updates.	Answer: A
2.	Five essential actions to follow for successful social media strategies include acknowledgement, reciprocation, personalization, promotion and repetition.	Answer: A
3.	Yahoo! Pipes allows you to automatically hashtag your content. (True)	Answer: A

4.	Once you've gotten your Twitter account on auto-pilot, you'll start receiving many more followers.	Answer: B Once you've put your Twitter account on auto-pilot through automated tweets, you still have to put forth the time and effort to publish original tweets and acknowledge your followers through #FollowFriday and @ mentions, for example.
5.	You cannot use Yahoo! Pipes in conjuction with Google Alerts and WordPress.alse	Answer: B This chapter has made extensive use of combining Yahoo! Pipes with Google Alerts and WordPress, so it is definitely doable.

Index

Thank you for buying
Social Media for WordPress

About Packt Publishing

Packt, pronounced 'packed', published its first book "*Mastering phpMyAdmin for Effective MySQL Management*" in April 2004 and subsequently continued to specialize in publishing highly focused books on specific technologies and solutions.

Our books and publications share the experiences of your fellow IT professionals in adapting and customizing today's systems, applications, and frameworks. Our solution based books give you the knowledge and power to customize the software and technologies you're using to get the job done. Packt books are more specific and less general than the IT books you have seen in the past. Our unique business model allows us to bring you more focused information, giving you more of what you need to know, and less of what you don't.

Packt is a modern, yet unique publishing company, which focuses on producing quality, cutting-edge books for communities of developers, administrators, and newbies alike. For more information, please visit our website: www.packtpub.com.

About Packt Open Source

In 2010, Packt launched two new brands, Packt Open Source and Packt Enterprise, in order to continue its focus on specialization. This book is part of the Packt Open Source brand, home to books published on software built around Open Source licences, and offering information to anybody from advanced developers to budding web designers. The Open Source brand also runs Packt's Open Source Royalty Scheme, by which Packt gives a royalty to each Open Source project about whose software a book is sold.

Writing for Packt

We welcome all inquiries from people who are interested in authoring. Book proposals should be sent to author@packtpub.com. If your book idea is still at an early stage and you would like to discuss it first before writing a formal book proposal, contact us; one of our commissioning editors will get in touch with you.

We're not just looking for published authors; if you have strong technical skills but no writing experience, our experienced editors can help you develop a writing career, or simply get some additional reward for your expertise.

Internet Marketing with WordPress

ISBN: 978-1-84951-674-7   Paperback: 112 pages

Use the power of WordPress to target customers, increase traffic, and build your business

1. Get practical experience in key aspects of online marketing

2. Accurately identify your business objectives and target audience to maximize your marketing efficiency

3. Create and deliver awesome SEO-enhanced, targeted content to drive large numbers of visitors through your blog

WordPress 3 Ultimate Security

ISBN: 978-1-84951-210-7   Paperback: 408 pages

Protect your WordPress site and its network

1. Know the risks, think like a hacker, use their toolkit, find problems first – and kick attacks into touch

2. Lock down your entire network from the local PC and web connection to the server and WordPress itself

3. Find out how to back up and secure your content and, when it's scraped, know what to do to enforce your copyright

4. Understand disaster recovery and use the best-of-breed tools, code, modules, techniques, and plugins to insure against attacks

Please check **www.PacktPub.com** for information on our titles

WordPress 3 For Business Bloggers

ISBN: 978-1-84951-132-2 Paperback: 346 pages

Promote and grow your WordPress blog with advanced marketing techniques, plugins, advertising, and SEO

1. Use WordPress to create a winning blog for your business

2. Develop and transform your blog with strategic goals

3. Market and measure the success of your blog

Responsive Web Design with HTML5 and CSS3

ISBN: 978-1-84969-318-9 Paperback: 325 pages

Learn responsive design using HTML5 and CSS3 to adapt websites to any browser or screen size

1. Everything needed to code websites in HTML5 and CSS3 that are responsive to every device or screen size

2. Learn the main new features of HTML5 and use CSS3's stunning new capabilities including animations, transitions and transformations

3. Real world examples show how to progressively enhance a responsive design while providing fall backs for older browsers

Please check **www.PacktPub.com** for information on our titles

www.ingramcontent.com/pod-product-compliance
Lightning Source LLC
Chambersburg PA
CBHW060141060326
40690CB00018B/3938